That W
Then

BUT THIS
IS NOW

To Fiona
Larga vida geografía!

best Wishes

Andy Griss

For Tania, Will and Tom

First Published in Great Britain in 2018 by DB Publishing,
an imprint of JMD Media Ltd

ISBN 978-1-78091-573-9

Printed and bound in the UK

That Was Then

BUT THIS IS NOW

Travels In Spain

ANDY GRIGG

ACKNOWLEDGEMENTS

Thanks to Tania, Will and Tom, without whom this book would not have been possible.

Thanks also to the following for their direct or indirect contributions towards this book:

Carmen Kilner; Miguel Ángel Del Arco Blanco; Paul Preston: Steve Caron; Dan Coxon; Grahame and Hilary Collyer: Stuart and Olwyn Mason; Jose María Hernández García; Ros Murray and Joe Strummer.

CONTENTS

FOREWORD

Throughout history, Spain has been the destiny for many travellers. It is not strange for a country placed in the southern limit of a continent like Europe, on the other side of another one like Africa, and bathed by two seas and one ocean. Indeed, the Iberian Peninsula had become the place for the encounter and flourishing of many cultures and societies. Then, from 19th century, Spain caught the attention of many Western visitors. Many romantic travellers from countries like France, England or even the United States came, attracted by an exotic image of our country. In the 20th century, many others travelled and lived in Spain, keeping some of these romantic ideas, but also interested by the political conflicts that took place in the interwar years that lead to the Spanish Civil War.

Probably the best example of this could be Gerald Brenan. He moved to the rural Alpujarras in the southern province of Granada in the 1920s, where he wrote many pages about Spanish culture and the social and political conflicts that originated the war in 1936. Every historian (and maybe every Spaniard) should appreciate the efforts done by Brenan to reflect the Spanish traditions and to grasp the causes of both the traumatic war and the terrible Francoist dictatorship that followed. Notwithstanding, it is also true that Brenan's writings are sometimes charged with a certain romantic tradition that assumes the 'backwardness' of Spain and the 'irrationalness' of Spaniards.

This is not the case with Andy Grigg's book, for which I have the honour of writing this foreword. His book is part of this tradition of foreign visitors who came attracted by the Spanish culture and history. However, although he admires and highlights the peculiarities that he sees, that idea of an archaic and backward country is surprisingly absent in his pages. It is not strange. First, Andy Grigg writes from the 21st century, and he belongs to a generation born after 1945 who did not live through World War Two or the postwar years. He was raised in the 1970s and the early 1980s, listening to (and loving) The Clash and The Smiths, and protesting against neoliberal policies carried out by Margaret Thatcher. Actually, he visited Spain for the first time in 1984, almost ten years after the death of the dictator. The author's biographical and historical context, but also his knowledge of Spanish history and his ability to perceive what he observes, enable him to offer a different image of the country in the recent years: 'Spain is a modern country with modern ambitions, but its soul is rooted deeply and firmly in the past.'

There are many books about the travel experience throughout Spain, but from my point of view, Andy Grigg's is a special one. The author carries the reader through his travels and experiences in Spain in two different historical moments. First, when he was young and he was just 20 years old; and secondly, in the trip that he would take two decades later in 2015 with his wife and his two sons, complementing the narration and his personal view of the country with its account. Thus, both moments overlap in his book, actually creating a 'double-text': while how Spain is today constitutes a description and a reflection of his experiences, the sections about his first visit to Spain are like a sort of memoir written from the present.

Second, I consider that the book will help the reader to get to know more about Spain, the Spaniards and our history. As always happens in every travel diary, this text is autobiographical. However, Andy Grigg always finds space to lead us through the most important aspects of the history of the places and monuments that he visits. It needs to be said that he does so in a completely precise and accurate way, providing information about such different aspects of Spanish history as the Phoenicians, the Romans, the Visigoths, Al-Andalus, the Catholic Monarchs and, of course, the Spanish Civil War. As both a Spaniard and a historian, I have to say that Andy Grigg has not only lived the country, but also read and learnt many things about it. And he knows how to transmit it.

It is also true that the book not only revolves around history: it contains aspects and personal experiences about modern Spain. Throughout its pages celebrated people parade, like Joe Strummer, coexisting with regular individuals, such as devout taxi drivers. Modern music is all around in every experience lived in the trip. And of course, Andy Grigg narrates some funny anecdotes of his experiences in the country, one being his first night in Málaga in 1984, which is simply hilarious.

Thirdly, I honestly think that the book is a perfect guide, not only to know about Spain and the Spaniards. It is also a fantastic opportunity to compare how Spain (and maybe other European southern countries like Portugal and Greece) has changed since the arrival of democracy in 1978 and its entering into the European Community. In every This Was Then section, Andy Grigg relates his shocking experiences with people in the years of 'La Movida', when traces of the old Spain coexisted in the country with the appearance of cultural renovation and the modernisation of the society. On the other hand, every And This is Now fragment helps us to know how the country has changed, and how sometimes the traveller has to be clever enough to escape from mass tourism to enjoy and live real Spain.

To conclude, there is a final aspect that emerges in the book. Andy Grigg is not just writing about Spain. He is also reflecting many human aspects that involve us all. While he narrates his travels through past and present Spain, he is defending the necessity to travel, to see, to know, and to experience. Thus, sometimes one has the impression that the book is partly an ode to travelling. For him, to travel is to live. The fact that the book, as we have already mentioned, is both a memory of his first visit to Spain and an account of his family visit evidences that travelling is not only a way of living, but also a way to remember, to enjoy the present and to face the future.

Miguel Ángel del Arco Blanco
Granada, 21 August 2018

DEPARTURES AND ARRIVALS
Youth versus Experience

That Was Then

'It is a truth universally acknowledged, that a single man in possession of a Spanish phrase book must be in want of a holiday.' Well, not necessarily! I didn't want a holiday, I wanted a life-changing experience. I wanted to immerse myself in the Spain of Hemingway, Laurie Lee and Orwell, I wanted to walk in the shadow of Lorca, Durruti and La Pasionaria, I wanted to soak up the intoxicating culture of a country shaped by religion, imagery, tradition, modernism and social realism; I also wanted to get drunk and meet Spanish girls.

Just over thirty years ago, as the miners went on strike and The Smiths released their first album, I left a trouble-torn Thatcherite Britain and boarded a flight for Malaga. Clutching my Spanish phrase book and a copy of *For Whom the Bell Tolls*, I dreamed of adventure. I was Robert Jordan, I was Hemingway, I was Joe Strummer. I was every self-obsessed left-wing student who has ever wanted to believe that they are anything other than a blind stereotype. In short, I was a modern-day Don Quixote, but with even less sense of reality. For a boy born in Devon, who had spent every summer holiday travelling almost thirty miles to Cornwall, the possibilities appeared to be endless. Today I look back and shudder, but I wouldn't swap the excitement and exhilaration of naive belief for anything cynicism can deliver.

Unfortunately, I can't remember many details of the flight to Spain, but I do remember the thrill of flying for the first time. I remember being transfixed by the beauty of a world seemingly turned upside down. The clouds below formed landscapes of ghostly mountains and valleys, illuminated by a blinding intensity of sunlight, seldom seen on a road trip to Cornwall. As I gazed and I read, I planned and I dreamed, and just when I thought things couldn't get any better I experienced another new reality: complimentary food and drinks. Heaven was indeed up here. As I read, I drank, and as I planned and dreamed I drank. I ate olives and spicy cold meats washed down by copious amounts of Rioja.

Shortly afterwards, overexcited, overindulged and over the limit, the plane began its final descent and I set foot on Spanish soil for the first time. With Hemingway under one arm, my phrase book in my pocket and a smile fuelled by anticipation and alcohol, I approached the terminal, collected my luggage and headed towards passport control.

Unfortunately, my level of intoxication singled me out for special treatment from airport security, ably supported by the local police. My passport was immediately confiscated, and I was subjected to the sort of interrogation that I presumed had died with Franco.

The adventure had begun.

THIS IS NOW

Thirty years on and I'm returning to the Spain of my youth, accompanied by my long-suffering wife, Tania, and my two sons, Will and Tom. I still carry a phrase book and I have Hemingway, Laurie Lee and Orwell downloaded on my Kindle. I still want to soak up the intoxicating culture of Spain, a country with real regional differences and divides, but a country with a shared life-affirming attitude and a country that embodies the spirit of *duende*, that heightened state of authenticity, expression and emotion, that for me is the essence of Spain. I still want to walk in the shadow of Lorca, Durutti and La Pasionaria, but I want to walk with Tania and the boys, and I might walk a little more slowly and circumspectly. I'm still excited and exhilarated, but I don't want a life-changing experience, I want a holiday.

I relax as much as I can in the cramped confines of a bucket list aircraft, and although I feel slightly cheated by the lack of any complimentary drinks or food, I hold on to the fact that at least I can keep a clear head. I chat to Tania and the boys, we plan and we dream. We talk about Seville, Cordoba, Ronda, Granada, and all the other places that we want to see and the things that we want to do. We talk about Spanish food, drink and culture, and I try to explain just what it is about Spain that makes me love the country so much. The boys' eyes glaze over and Tania yawns, I take the hint and I start to read *Homage to Catalonia*, Orwell's account of his part in the Spanish Civil War. I read for a while, then I put down my Kindle and plug in my earphones. I gaze down at the clouds, and with the words of 'Spanish Bombs' by The Clash circling around my head, I'm remembering not the days of '39, but the days of '84.

That Was Then

'*Que estás haciendo en España? Cuánto tiempo te quedarás? Por qué estás aquí? Donde estan las drogas?*'

It's amazing just how quickly you can sober up when armed police ask you questions. My head began to clear and I listened more intently than I had ever listened to a language lesson at school, but I could still only understand a fraction of what was being said. My lack of comprehension obviously frustrated my interrogators, who appeared to be having a bad day. My luggage was searched, my pockets were turned out and I thought I saw a pair of rubber gloves out of the corner of my eye. Entering Cornwall can sometimes be a scary, but this was beyond the pale. I tried my own questions, in my own version of Spanglish, but I received no reply, and to be fair my Spanish was so bad that they probably didn't have a clue what I was talking about.

The questions continued, my passport – which had been confiscated – was now taken away from the small, enclosed stuffy room, which I imagined could be my final resting place. I really shouldn't have watched *Midnight Express* just before travelling.

At one time, temporarily left on my own, I remembered my phrase book, but I couldn't find out how to say, 'I'm British and I want to phone the embassy.' My captors returned, the questions continued, my mumbled responses grew even less coherent, anxiety turned to fear. I was supposed to be meeting my girlfriend at arrivals, but would I ever arrive?

In total I was held for just over three hours, at which point my passport was returned and without any explanation I was finally allowed to enter Spain.

The airport was practically deserted, but Ariana was patiently waiting for me. I felt tired, stressed and hungover. I definitely regretted the last and possibly the penultimate drink that I had had on the plane and I now felt extremely dehydrated. After greeting Ariana, and feeling slightly aggrieved that stories of my recent experience received nothing more than a shrug of the shoulder and a cry of 'Well, it's Spain, what do you expect?', we decided to take a train and head into the city.

After booking a room close to The Maria Zambrano train station in Malaga, we wandered out into the Spanish night. Disregarding ambience and architecture, I wandered out with one aim in mind: I needed to quench my insufferable thirst. In the early eighties, xenophobia trumped common sense in terms of travel advice; all advice had the hint of a *Daily Mail* editorial about it. Whenever and wherever you travelled, you mustn't under any circumstances drink the tap water.

'*Hay un bar por aquí?*' I asked. My question was met with a polite response and a string of directions that I just about managed to translate, '*dereche*', '*izquierda*' and '*todo recto*'. Twisting and turning through narrow streets, we soon arrived at a neon-lit bar, or 'Nite Club' as the sign proclaimed.

On first inspection the bar looked like just any other bar, but how all the customers stared. Maybe it was me? Dressed to thrill (nobody but myself), with high hair and a style that paid homage to every miserable rock star that ever wore black. I ignored the looks and bought a drink.

The drinks were cheap enough and I immediately felt revived. However, as I looked around, I began to sense that the cliental conformed to a certain type. The '*mujeres*' were all dressed in a style that, whilst pleasing to the eye, didn't seem particularly traditional. Leather and plastic, low-cut tops, extremely short skirts and flesh dominated the scene. Many of the men were suited and booted, and looked like extras from an Andalusian version of *The Godfather*. Oh well, eyes down, a couple of drinks and then back to the hotel.

A couple of drinks later and with no intention of heading back to the hotel, I headed for the toilets. I sauntered down a long narrow corridor with toilets at one end and multiple doorways in between. One door was open.

Revealed was a small, seedy-looking bedroom; the peseta was beginning to drop.

Thinking that we should probably quit and return to the hotel, I returned to Ariana, but she was engaged in a heated conversation. 'I've just been propositioned,' she said. 'How much?' I nearly asked, before thinking better of it.

Making our excuses in typically English style (although my girlfriend was Spanish), we wished a pleasant '*buenas noches*' to the prostitutes, pimps and clients, and headed for home.

THIS IS NOW

I grip my passport tightly as sweat breaks out and begins to trickle down the back of my neck. Do I smile and look directly at the passport officials? Or do I look away and avoid eye contact? In my present mindset, both scenarios appear fraught with danger. If I smile, they might think that I'm trying to bluff them, and if I look away they might see it as admission of guilt. 'What's up Dad? You look worried.' 'Nothing, it's just that the past is sometimes a difficult place to visit.' Will looks confused and obviously regrets his question, I stand in line, feeling and probably looking like a condemned man.

'Welcome to Spain, *señor*.'

Waves of relief spread through me as I cradle my rucksack and the carefully hidden ten grams of resin that lie within. Don't worry, I'm joking. I really don't know why I was quite so worried, but the past has a strong grip on all of us and just like many others when faced with officialdom, I always feel guilty of something.

No train transfer to Malaga this time around, but a hire car, courtesy of 'Auto Navarro' and booked through a friend of a colleague. 'What's great is that the cars are all so reliable,' I was unreliably informed.

I'm at risk of getting slightly ahead of myself, because initially everything went to plan. We were delighted to meet a man at arrivals holding up a sign with our name on it. It's great when a plan comes together. We followed our one-man welcome party as he led us out of the main airport terminal and through a maze of car parks. The welcome could have been a little more effusive and ebullient, but I suppose we were on holiday and he wasn't. Our new companion appeared to be on the bleak side of miserable, like a Thomas Hardy character who was having a worse day than normal. He was fairly taciturn and didn't even laugh at my Spanish one-liners. Of course, it is just possible that he was at the end of a long and busy shift, and it's also possible that he didn't understand a single word that I was trying to say. I had spent a considerable amount of time, money and energy trying to improve my Spanish, but I think I might have required considerably more time, money and energy and at least some natural linguistic ability.

Reduced to silence, we made it to the car. Thinking to myself 'must remember to drive on the right', we packed our luggage into our truly unremarkable Nissan Note, waved '*adiós*' to '*el hombre desdichado*', and headed off towards Seville.

ANDALUSIA

That Was Then

Home was a rather old and neglected-looking hotel in downtown Malaga. The hotel hadn't been selected for its level of opulence, reputation or quality of service, but for its cost effectiveness. 'El Nite Club' had looked more inviting. I have forgotten the name of the hotel, but I haven't forgotten the lack of welcome, comfort or cleanliness. Nevertheless, my thirst had been satiated, I was on holiday, I was in Spain and I was determined to enjoy myself. Thinking that I should re-engage with ambience and architecture, I decided to gaze out over the illuminated city streets of Malaga, before heading to bed. Our room was on the fifth floor and I fully expected the views to be impressive. I headed towards where I thought a window should be, but I was disappointed. What I thought was a curtain turned out to be a faded wall hanging. I paced around the room, I investigated all four walls, but there was no window to be found, not even a skylight. We hadn't paid much for the room, but we really didn't think that a window would be an optional extra. Further investigation revealed that we were staying in a box room that had been split off from another room at some earlier stage in the ancient building's history. 'Oh well,' I thought to myself: being detained at customs, accidentally visiting a brothel and staying in 'a room without a view' might not be the most encouraging way to start a holiday, but tomorrow was another day, and tomorrow I would be exploring Andalusia.

Andalusia

In the early 1980s I developed a love of all things Spanish: history, culture, politics, food and drink, but I had little real knowledge of Andalusia. The reason that I arrived in Andalusia in 1984, rather than any other region of Spain, was that my girlfriend was studying in Granada. The reason why I was returning with my family was because Andalusia encapsulates all that is the best of Spain: a rich long history, a unique culture, political fervour and fantastic food and drink.

15

   Many of the 'things' that we think of as being typically Spanish, are largely or entirely Andalusian in origin: flamenco, bullfighting, tapas and Moorish-influenced architectural styles, to name but a few. Andalusia is also hot – maybe too hot for some, but I rarely leave the UK searching for cold or wet weather. Andalusia is the hottest area in Europe and daytime highs of over forty degrees centigrade are not uncommon.

Andalusia possesses a wonderful and varied landscape. If you really want to, it's possible to ski in the morning and swim in the afternoon. Alpine mountains and pine forests can be explored, as well as barren deserts, fertile irrigated plains and sun-kissed beaches. Andalusia really has got something for everyone, and everything for me.

One common misconception held about Spain is that it's a flat country. 'The rain in Spain' may 'fall mainly on the plain', but Spain is one of the most mountainous countries in Europe. In Andalusia, mountain ranges run from the south-west to the north-east. The Sierra Morena is the northernmost range and it crosses the northern parts of Huelva, Seville, Cordoba and Jean. The Sierra Morena is high, desolate and rarely visited, but it did provide a refuge for Don Quixote and Sancho Panza. In the south-east, the Sierra Nevada or 'Snowy Range', part of the Baetic Cordillera, contains the highest mountains in the country, rising to well over 3,000 metres. The mountains provide great opportunities to walk and explore largely unexplored areas.

Between the two ranges of mountains lie the Guadalquivir River basin and its fertile plains. The river flows south-west across almost the whole of Andalusia, passing through the cities of Cordoba and Seville, before emptying into the Atlantic Ocean west of Cadiz. The lower basin of the river, La Campina, is the most densely settled part of Andalusia, while an arid barren area covers much of Granada and Almeria. Extending east and west of Malaga is the Costa del Sol. Whilst it's true that many of the coastal resorts are overdeveloped and overcrowded, some resorts still offer idyllic locations to rest and relax in.

Another major 'pull' factor when it comes to Andalusia is its history. The name 'Andalusia' is thought to derive from the Arabic word *Al-Andalus*, and this word is thought to derive from an even older word, *Vandalusia* or 'land of the Vandals'. The long history of the area is a direct consequence of Andalusia's important geographical location, providing as it does a gateway into Europe from Africa. Andalusia has been influenced and settled by Iberians, Phoenicians, Carthaginians, Romans, Vandals, Visigoths, Muslims and Castilians. This variety of influences has shaped the landscape, the people and the culture of modern-day Andalusia. Andalusia is very much a product of its past. To fully understand the present, that past needs to be told.

Settled societies first developed in Andalusia about 6,000 years ago, then (at least in terms of this brief history) not much happened for the next 3,000 years.

Fast-forwarding through time, around 900 BC the mineral and agricultural wealth of the indigenous people attracted the interest of Phoenician traders. The Phoenicians confirmed their interest by establishing trading colonies on coastal sites such as Cadiz, Huelva and Malaga. In the 8th and 7th centuries BC, Phoenician influence declined and this gave rise to the mysterious and semi-mythical Tartessus civilisation, mentioned by Greek and Roman sources and seen by some as being synonymous with Atlantis. The decline of Phoenician influence throughout the whole of the Mediterranean led to the emergence of Carthage (a former Phoenician city state) as the predominant force in the area. Carthage went on to colonise the coastal area of what is now Andalusia, but the might of Carthage brought them into direct conflict with that other rising power of the Mediterranean, the Romans. The Romans, led by Scipio Africanus, conquered Andalusia between 210 and 206 BC, and the region eventually became the Roman province of Baetica. Thriving under Roman rule, Andalusia was the birthplace of the emperors Trajan and Hadrian. In Roman times, Andalusia was governed from Cordoba; it was one of the wealthiest and most civilised areas of the Roman Empire. Rome imported Andalusian products such as olives, copper, silver and fish. Roman rule lasted until the Vandals (remember Vandalusia, hence the name Andalusia) and then the Visigoths overran the region in the 5th century AD.

The Visigothic kingdom lasted for just over 300 years, but by the 8th century AD the kingdom was tearing itself apart. In short, a very uncivil civil war broke out. The weakened state of the Visigothic kingdom, combined with expanding Muslim influence in North Africa, paved the way for the Muslim conquest of Spain. It is believed that Muslims were initially invited into Andalusia by one of the feuding Visigothic parties, but after discovering how weak the defences were, and after defeating and virtually destroying the Visigoths at the Battle of Guadalete (Rio Barbate) in 711, the Umayyad Arab armies moved north to take full advantage of the situation. Initially some 10,000 men, mostly Berbers (indigenous North Africans) under the leadership of Tariq ibn Ziyad, crossed the Strait of Gibraltar from Tangier (now in Morocco) and entered Andalusia. Subsequently (for about the next 700 years), Andalusia's history was interlinked with that of the North African coast. To some extent the invasion may have been opportunistic, but it is thought by many eminent scholars that after the conquest of North Africa, the Muslim invasion and conquest of Andalusia was a logical and an almost inevitable step. Apart from adding Andalusia to the Arab Empire, Andalusia would act as a base for further expansion into Europe.

Initially Cordoba, then Seville and finally Granada, took turns as being the leading city of Islamic Spain. At its peak in the 10th century, Cordoba was the biggest, the grandest, the most dazzling and the most cultured city in the known world.

The Arabic name Al-Andalus was originally applied by the Muslims (Moors) to the entire Iberian Peninsula. However, in the 11th century, when the Christians began to reconquer the peninsula, Al-Andalus, or Andalusia, came to mean only that area still under Muslim control.

After the Muslim conquest, Andalusia became part of the independent Umayyad caliphate of Cordoba, which was founded in AD 929. After the breakup of this unified Spanish Muslim state in the early 11th century, Andalusia was divided into a number of small kingdoms or *tarifas*, the largest of which were Malaga, Seville and Cordoba. Eventually (and once again almost inevitably) another uncivil civil war broke out and the *tarifas*, suitably weakened by infighting, began falling to Christian forces based in Leon and Castile. However, in the 11th century a new Muslim invasion from North Africa, that of the Berber Almoravids, once again established centralised rule over Muslim Spain. The Almoravids were in turn succeeded by another force of Muslim invaders from North Africa, a militant sect called the Almohads. The Almohads ruled over Andalusia from about 1147–1212.

The Moorish period is often seen as the golden age of Andalusia, because of its economic prosperity and its cultural awakening. Agriculture, mining and industry flourished as never before, and the region carried on a rich trade with North Africa. Some of the crops grown in Andalusia today, such as sugarcane, almonds and apricots, were introduced by the Arabs, and much of the region's elaborate irrigation system dates from the Muslim period. In terms of culture and learning, a vibrant civilisation arose out of the intermingling of Berber and Arab Muslims, alongside Spanish Christians and Jews, under the relatively tolerant rule of the Muslim emirs. An unprecedented fusion of belief and thought accelerated knowledge and development. The cities of Cordoba, Seville and Granada became celebrated centres of Muslim architecture, science and learning, at a time when the rest of Europe was still emerging from the Dark Ages. The great Mosque of Cordoba and the fortress-palace of the Alhambra in

Granada were built during this period. Today, these are two of the most popular tourist attractions in Europe.

The Almohad's power in southern Spain disintegrated after their defeat by Christian armies led by King Alfonso VIII of Castile at the Battle of Las Navas de Tolosa in 1212. The small Muslim states that re-emerged after this period were unable to mount a unified resistance to Christian reconquest. By 1251, Ferdinand III of Castile had reconquered all of Andalusia, except the Muslim kingdom of Granada, which survived until its capture by the united forces of Ferdinand II of Aragon and Isabella I of Castile in 1492.

1492 also marks the date when Columbus landed in Hispaniola, paving the way for the Conquistadors and the conquest of the Americas. Wealth from the New World flooded into Spain via the ports of Cadiz and Seville, ensuring the continued prosperity of Andalusia. However, the expulsion of the Moriscos (Christianised Muslims) from Spain in 1609 helped trigger an economic decline, that accelerated when Seville and Cadiz lost their trading monopolies with the New World in the 18th century.

Economic decline led to extreme poverty, which enveloped the whole region, producing hardship for the majority of the people. By the late 19th century, poverty and destitution in rural Andalusia meant that it was receptive to the ideas of left-wing ideologists, anarchists and social reformers. During the Spanish Civil War, Andalusia split along class lines and savage atrocities were committed by both sides. Franco's rebels (supported by Hitler and the full military might of Nazi Germany) eventually triumphed and Spain's subsequent 'hungry years' were particularly hungry in Andalusia.

Since the death of Franco, and Spain's re-emergence into modern Europe, an economic boom based on construction and tourism has been followed by recession and decline. Today, unemployment in Andalusia is higher than in any other area of Spain, but Andalusians are resilient and philosophical, they have seen it all before and ultimately, they believe that life is to be lived to the full. The spirit of *duende* lives on.

THIS IS NOW

Leaving the airport, we joined the main road to Seville. Settling into our journey, we looked forward to the holiday ahead. The beginning of any holiday should be a joyous moment; the whole holiday lies before you and if it's going to be a disaster, well, you don't know it yet. The start of any holiday is a time for real optimism.

After travelling for about an hour, feeling outwardly optimistic, but inwardly expecting the worst, we surrendered to hunger and stopped at a roadside service station. From the outside the building was less than inspiring: a modern concrete edifice that promised nothing and gave the impression that it would deliver less. Inside, however, we were delighted to discover a traditionally styled 'taberna', complete with hanging hams and delightfully tasty tapas.

Ordering some food and fighting the urge to order a cerveza, Tom suddenly asked 'Why Andalusia, Dad? Why is it so special?' As we waited for our food to arrive, I began to explain to anyone who cared to listen just why I consider Andalusia to be so special. I skipped over some details, but eyes glazed over as I got carried away by my own musings. Once again, I got the distinct feeling that my children often regret asking me questions.

Apart from the near mutiny instigated by my musings, the journey from Malaga to the outskirts of Seville went largely without incident. Despite what many people say, the Spanish drive well. They may not be particularly tolerant of other drivers' mistakes, but by and large they drive safely and according to recognised conventions. In my acceptably limited experience, the worst drivers of all live in Cyprus. Most Cypriots appear to have developed a type of colour blindness; they can't seem to be able to distinguish between red and green. Speed limits are almost universally ignored and drivers suddenly divert from their onward path, stopping and parking with a level of abruptness that is downright dangerous.

The journey from Malaga to the outskirts of Seville may have gone well, but the journey from the outskirts to the centre of Seville didn't go so smoothly. With the satnav on the blink, patience in short supply and divorce lawyers on standby, our hotel seemed a long way away.

FIRST IMPRESSIONS
Seville

That Was Then

As soon as I opened my eyes, I immediately wished I hadn't. All I could see were vertiginous slopes leading down to a dry valley, hundreds of feet below. Staring into the abyss I felt strangely drawn to the depths. I was terrified, but I couldn't avert my gaze. Last night I had wanted a view, now I most definitely had one. I felt sure that the drop was getting ready to welcome me, but suddenly the drop disappeared. Stone and then tarmac filled my line of vision. The coach had swung to the left and I was able to blink again. Turning my head, I saw a broken crash barrier and a bunch of withered flowers attached to a faded photograph and a cross. I had been right to be worried. In 1984, a coach trip from Malaga to the interior was not for the faint-hearted.

THIS IS NOW

One minute I was happily singing along to 'The Bullfighter Dies' by Morrissey (a song that perhaps shouldn't be sung out loud in Andalusia), and then the next minute the satnav lost all links to reality as we hit the confusion of Seville central. I may not have been 'ill in Seville', but tensions were high and stress levels soared.

If my experience is anything to go by (which it usually isn't), then I think satnavs have probably saved many a marriage. Tania is a fantastic planner and organiser and most of our trips and holidays are down to her organisational ability; however, a sense of direction is not one of her strongest suits. Directional dyslexia, primarily an inability to distinguish right from left, has caused many a tense moment. It's not even a fifty-fifty situation. Ninety per cent of the time Tania makes the wrong call, but it's that ten per cent chance of accuracy that makes all directional pronouncements the source of disbelief and confusion. Accuracy was important today. We were booked to stay in a hotel located within the myriad of narrow and mostly pedestrianised streets that make up Seville's Jewish quarter.

We trusted our satnav as it sent us on a twisted journey through narrow streets and alleys, but our trust was misplaced. The satnav was seemingly confused by the one-way system and the tall buildings which intermittently blocked digital communications. Overshooting a right turn, we lost our way; it was time for manual navigation to take over. 'Right here, no left, I mean right.' Now we were well and truly lost. Mystified about our own whereabouts, the satnav briefly returned to life and authoritatively commanded us to turn into a pedestrianised plaza; panic reigned supreme. Once again, sweat trickled down the back of my neck as I grasped the steering wheel tightly and looked for anywhere, just anywhere to park. 'Coach trips aren't this stressful' I thought to myself, before remembering that they are.

Fortunately, I spotted a parking place. Stopping outside a hotel (unfortunately not ours), we did the unthinkable: we asked for directions. Minutes later, we parked in a small underground car park on the edge of the Jewish quarter. We ignored the high parking charges, correctly surmising that we wouldn't find anything cheaper and correctly realising that the relief of arrival would be an almost priceless experience.

We were correct.

Feeling simultaneously both calm and elated, we completed a short walk and arrived at the Murillo Hotel. The hotel was somewhat grander than my half-forgotten hotel in Malaga. The entrance was guarded by two armoured knights, who mutely and motionlessly greeted our arrival. The entrance lobby was spectacular: hand-carved furniture and beautifully ornate *objets d'art* nestled under an intricately carved and inlaid wooden ceiling. Another welcome change from my previous experience was that the staff were both helpful and friendly. After handing over our passports and exchanging pleasantries, they pointed the way to our air-conditioned rooms. Air conditioning is a blessing in Spain. Without air conditioning the still air and incessant heat of summer mean that sleep is almost impossible. The sultry conditions drive people out onto the streets until the coolness of late night or early dawn makes slumber a viable option. Enforced exodus, however, isn't an entirely bad thing. Late-night multigenerational gatherings are one of the real joys of Spain.

Driven into the streets, not by heat or even really thirst, but by the pure excitement of arrival, we dropped off our luggage, switched on the air conditioning and visited a small bar immediately opposite the hotel. Ignoring our predetermined plan to siesta between three-thirty and five-thirty in the afternoon (the warmest part of the Andalusian day), we sank a drink and soaked up the atmosphere of Spain. We had already been in the country for over five hours, but it felt like we had finally arrived.

Excited and momentarily energised, we resisted the temptation for one cerveza to become two and forced ourselves to return to the hotel. We had been awake since four in the morning and correctly assumed that we needed a few hours' rest before venturing out to explore the city. Alternating between dozing and planning and sleeping and dreaming in our now cooled rooms, we avoided the heat of the afternoon and stored up our strength and energy for the night ahead.

Emerging rested and revived a few hours later, we began to explore Seville. I live in the countryside, so any city is a delight. I love the peace and quiet of the countryside, but that doesn't mean that I don't relish the crowded streets, the busy shops and the full and frantic bars and restaurants of a city in full swing. In lots of ways, my enjoyment of the urban experience is intensified by its uniqueness and brevity. Seville was not to be a disappointment.

Seville's Jewish quarter is a real labyrinth; a maze of narrow streets, thankfully shaded by tall and elegant buildings. Turning right and then left, with only a vague plan, we were now happy to get lost. Each twist and turn revealed fresh delight upon fresh delight. We walked down narrow ancient streets and alleyways and we walked through beautiful gardens, lined with Moroccan-style benches. We walked next to the crenelated walls of the Alcazar, the sight of which afforded tantalising glimpses of the beauty that lies within. We walked through a network of seemingly blind alleyways, avoiding dead ends and passing beneath half-hidden archways. We gazed at the beauty of the cathedral and the dizzying heights of the Giralda Tower. We headed to the banks of the Guadalquivir, via the Plaza de Toros de la Maestranza, and crossed the river by way of the Puente de Isabel II. We stopped for a drink at one of the numerous riverside bars before returning to the east bank by way of the Puente de San Telmo, crossing close to the Torre del Oro.

We walked past so many stunning buildings that I began to wonder why, in more recent times, we seem to have lost the art of great architecture. How much more elegant and beautiful are the exquisitely crafted and regal buildings of yesteryear, compared to the majority of high-rise and high-yield buildings of today?

As we walked and we talked and we admired the architectural delights, we also looked out for somewhere to eat. Hunger had struck fairly early on our walk, but with over 300 bars to choose from, choice was a difficult thing. We were reluctant to settle for second best in a city of such culinary delights. We walked past many tempting bars, tabernas and restaurants, looking out for that one extra-special place that might be just around the next corner. An endless pursuit of excellence in a city where even the mediocre is tasty is a difficult and tiring thing to do.

Inevitably, after circling almost the entire city, we ended up at one of the first bars we had walked past.

Elegantly situated in a small square beneath an orange tree, we had found our own culinary nirvana. *Solomillo al whiskey, jamón iberico, gambas al ajillo, bacalao, calamares*, *chipirones*, *patatas bravas*, *tortilla*, *revuelto* and many other tasty dishes fought for our attention. We gave in to gluttony and ordered a mixture of different tapas to share. The joy of tapas is that you get to taste a variety of small and tasty dishes; it's actually not gluttony, it's culinary ecstasy.

There are a number of theories as to the origin of eating small snacks with drinks. Legend would have us believe that because of illness, the 13th-century Castilian King Alfonso X (The Wise) had to eat small snacks with his wine between meals to maintain his strength. After recovering from his illness, he passed a law that wine or beer served in tabernas had to be accompanied by food. However, it's more likely that the origins were practical, with bread or a small plate of ham or olives being used to keep dust or insects out of drinks (the literal meaning of 'tapa' is 'lid'). It was also the custom for agricultural and other manual workers to eat small snacks so that they could continue working until the main meal of the day arrived. Tapas in its modern form is generally believed to have begun in the tabernas and bars of Seville – perhaps in the bar in which we now sat.

Feeling both full and satisfied, we watched the shadows lengthen as the sun set and '*la noche*' closed in. As the cool of the evening replaced the heat of the day, we realised that it was one of those evenings that you never want to end. We walked back to the main cathedral square, gazing at the illuminated beauty of a city which had now come fully to life. Excited but tired, we then returned to the bar outside the hotel for what we thought would be one final drink. The cool, elegant and delicious orange-infused wine (*vino naranja*) temporarily satisfied our thirst for yet more Spanish experiences. Tania and I decided, however, that one final drink wasn't quite enough. Although the hour was late it was too early to stop. We sent the boys to bed and headed to the terrace bar, perched on the roof of our hotel.

What could be better, a final, final drink, in the cool of the night, overlooking the breathtakingly beautiful city of Seville. Feeling just about as contented as life allows, I gazed at the illuminated city streets and the grandiose Giralda Tower – an incandescent beacon of magnificence.

Today we had experienced the beauty of Seville from the streets. Tomorrow we would delve behind walls, closed doors and entrance fees, and we would hopefully discover an inner beauty to this city of outward delights.

FIRST IMPRESSIONS
Granada

That Was Then

I could hear it before I could see it, but I could only guess as to what was happening. Perhaps it was a riot, or perhaps a street brawl had broken out. A cacophony of voices echoed down the street, getting louder as we reached the corner of the square. I slowed my pace accordingly, apprehensive about what was to come next. It had been another eventful day and my nerves were only just recovering from the coach trip from Malaga. As we turned the corner, I witnessed a crowd of animated people standing outside a small bar. On first inspection it looked like an angry mob. However, although voices were raised and people argued, there were no looks of anger or aggression, just smiles and occasional bursts of raucous laughter accompanied by frantic hand gestures and plumes of smoke. This was Spain, and this was a Spanish bar, and this was street life in Granada.

Pushing our way through the crowds, I forced my way into the bar and went to order a drink. 'Order wine,' Ariana shouted. *'Es muy barato'.* The bar was packed, but the immaculately dressed barmen were well trained; they noticed each and every new arrival and served all in a strict order which paid no favours and was effortlessly efficient. Orders were shouted and drinks were delivered with speed and dexterity, but this wasn't a bar for procrastinators or for the faint-hearted. Everything happened at top speed and high volume. God help you if you didn't know what you wanted to drink or you had come out expecting a quiet and peaceful evening. I loved the place. *'Dos vinos tintos,'* I asked, utilising one of my more useful Spanish phrases. The bar itself was basic but brilliant. The bar top was a glistening strip of aluminium, constantly polished by the barmen so it reflected their artistry; the walls were covered in ceramic tiles and mirrors, hams hung from the ceiling and sunflower seeds crunched underfoot on the floor below; images of days and owners gone by decorated the walls and various types of tapas were displayed with a pride that defied prejudice. The wine appeared, accompanied by a plate of mixed olives. 'How much?' I asked. The barmen looked confused. *'Cuánto es?'* I tried. The barman looked even more confused. 'You don't pay now, you pay at the end of the night or when you leave,' I was reliably informed by Ariana. Putting my money away, I looked for a seat, but there were just a few barstools and they had all been taken. 'Why is it so packed? Is it a special occasion?' I shouted, in an attempt to make myself heard over the general din of the place. 'It's Spain, this is normal,' Ariana replied.

This was Spain, and if this was normal I was delighted, because this was the Spain I had come to see. Lorca, Durruti and La Pasionaria would have been proud. Hemingway, Laurie Lee and Orwell would have joined in. Franco was dead and gone and a new, expressive and modernising left-wing Spain had emerged from the ashes of fascism. The Spanish Socialist Workers Party (PSOE), which had been banned by Franco, had come to power in 1982; they were the first left-wing party to hold power in Spain for forty-three years. Repression belonged to the past and new freedoms had arrived. Laws on drinks, drugs and censorship had all been relaxed. Spain was embracing modernity with a passion and the Spanish were making up for lost time. The pain of Francoism was an anachronism and a new pleasure principle had taken its place.

It's hard to get your head around the fact that an essentially fascist power, that had supported and been supported by Hitler, could have survived in

Europe until 1975. It's frightening to think that in a modernising Europe, Franco's regime continued to commit terrible atrocities right up until his death, while the rest of the world looked on. It's almost inconceivable to think, but when Heinrich Himmler visited Spain in 1940, a year after Franco's victory, he was shocked by the brutality of the Falangists (Franco's right-wing party). Summary executions of left-wing sympathisers were part and parcel of Franco's regime. Opponents of the dictatorship were brought before military courts to meet their fate. Repressive laws were issued, including the Law of Political Responsibilities, the Law of Security (which regarded alternative views or labour strikes as military rebellion) and the Law for the Repression of Masonry and Communism.

Political parties and trade unions were banned, except of course the government party and the government trade unions. Thousands of militants and supporters of the parties and trade unions declared illegal under Franco's dictatorship, such as the Spanish Socialist Workers' Party, the Communist Party of Spain (PCE), the Workers' General Union (UGT) and the National Confederation of Labour (CNT), were imprisoned or executed. Under Franco's determined vision to create a one nation state, regional languages such as Basque and Catalan were forbidden and the statutes of autonomy of Catalonia and the Basque Country were abolished. Censorship of the press and of cultural life was rigorously exercised and forbidden books were destroyed.

Estimates suggest that between 50,000 and 150,000 executions took place under Franco's rule and nearly half a million people were imprisoned in concentration camps. Prisoners were sent to work in militarised penal colonies and penal detachments. Prisoners of war were basically slaves of the state, forced to work on construction projects and in coal mining. Thousands died as a result of the appalling conditions that they had to live and work in; many died building Franco's own mausoleum, 'The Valley of the Fallen'.

The children of so-called 'undesirables', or left-wing sympathisers, could be taken away from their parents and brought up by Francoist families; many mothers were executed shortly after their children were taken away. Extensive purges were carried out amongst the civil service; some teachers and universities lecturers lost their lives, many lost their jobs; army officers, loyal to the Republic, were expelled from the army and priority for employment was always given to Nationalist supporters.

Franco's Spain had no conception or understanding of women's rights. Women required their husband's permission in order to take a job or open a bank account. Adultery by a woman was a crime, but adultery by a man was not. Divorce and marriage legislation was retroactively reversed; divorces were annulled and the children of civil marriages were deemed illegitimate.

Morality was under the governance of the Roman Catholic Church, who sat back and watched as atrocities mounted.

This was the Spain that the Spanish were now reacting against. A country that had effectively been a dictatorship, standing still while the rest of the world turned. The majority of Spaniards were ripe for revolution; a cultural and social revolution of the soul. People of all ages were probably filling bars of all types, all over Spain.

Downing a few more wines, I felt myself warming to Spain, the Spanish and life in general. I hadn't yet visited the centre of the city or seen the Alhambra or the Albaicin, but I already knew that I was going to love Granada. Heading back to the bar, I ordered two beers. The barman looked confused. 'Dos cervezas,' I shouted. The barman said something and pointed to my left, but I couldn't catch his meaning. 'Cervezas,' I repeated. Shrugging his shoulders, the barman put down the glasses he was cleaning, walked out from behind the bar, placed his hand on my shoulder and guided me to one side of the room. Initially confused, I found myself standing outside the toilets. 'Servicios,' he said. Now I understood. Regretting my poor grasp of Spanish pronunciation, I thanked my guide, stepped inside the toilets, waited for an appropriate amount of time to pass and then went back to the bar and ordered two wines. Fortunately I wasn't hungry, so I didn't ask for chicken.

SEVILLE
Second Thoughts

THIS IS NOW

It often takes a while to find your bearings in a new city. Initial arrival can conjure up memories of your first day at school; places are new and unfamiliar and everything looks impossibly large and hopelessly confusing. However, when you do find your bearings (maybe without any wider geographical knowledge or understanding of the city that you are in) you start to feel and act like a seasoned traveller, and you may even begin to look down on newer arrivals as they aimlessly scurry about dragging their suitcases behind them. How superior it feels to be able to stride out unencumbered by luggage, with at least some sense of direction and purpose.

Waking refreshed and revived after a comfortable air-conditioned night's sleep, we headed out for breakfast. Striding out confidently and with a keen sense of direction, we went the wrong way and couldn't find the cafe we had earmarked for breakfast the night before. However, with so many places to choose from we soon found a suitable spot. We enjoyed cafe con leche, *zumo* and croissants (not particularly Spanish, I know) accompanied by blasts of cool water vapour. The water vapour emanated from a sprinkler system attached to the front of the cafe – cool thinking in one of Europe's hottest cities. Breakfast was cheap and tasty and proved to be a great antidote to the previous day's travelling. It was strange to think that only yesterday we had woken up in Devon at four in the morning, yet we had ended the day drinking on a terrace bar overlooking Seville. It had been a long and tiring day, but a day full of excitement and new experiences. Sometimes you can pack an incredible amount into twenty-four hours, whilst on other occasions it's an effort just to get out of bed.

Having already made the effort to get out of bed and have breakfast, we decided that today was another day that we should pack full of new experiences. Pushing cups and plates to one side, we spread out our tourist map and started to plan our itinerary. With so much to see and do, we understood that planning was going to be difficult. Seville is the fourth largest city in Spain, and the Old

Town, the fourth largest in Europe, is a tangle of alleyways and ancient ways packed with fantastic places and amazing architecture. The Old Town includes three UNESCO World Heritage sites, two of which were high on our list of things to do. It's impossible to see and do everything in a large city with a long history, so we knew that we would have to be selective.

Seville is the capital of Andalusia and lies on the plain of the Guadalquivir River. Known in Roman times as Hispalis, Seville has been home to Vandals,

Visigoths and Moors. Whilst Roman remains can still be found in the city, it's the Moorish legacy that most people come to see. The Alcazar, the city walls and the Giralda (the bell tower of Seville Cathedral) are said to capture the imagination and the soul of the city. The Alcazar was one of the UNESCO sites that we were determined to visit. After the defeat of the Moorish forces, Seville continued to flourish under the Christian kings. One unique aspect of Seville is that it's Spain's only inland river port; this proved to be of great importance after the discovery of the Americas. As a consequence of its position, Seville monopolised trade with the New World, and a golden age of art and literature, based on great wealth and power, began. One consequence of this period was the completion of the truly colossal Seville Cathedral. The cathedral was another UNESCO site on our list of things to do and places to see. Seville was the place 'to see and be seen in' in the 16th century, the very centre of the world. As if to prove this point, in 1519 Magellan left Seville to complete the first circumnavigation of the Earth. In the 17th century, Seville reached its zenith, consolidating its power and wealth before a gradual economic, social and cultural decline set in, largely due to the silting up of the Guadalquivir River. Thinking that we should capture the moment before any of us began to decline, we formulated a plan and headed off towards the cathedral, but we took a circuitous route.

We decided to head to the cathedral via the Antigua Fabrica de Tabacos, or Old Tobacco Factory. The building was where Carmen worked as a cigar maker in Bizet's famous opera. The doomed heroine, a hot-blooded *cigarrera*, is still for many the incarnation of Spanish passion. Bizet's opera was based on an earlier story, but the inspiration for that story was the Antigua de Fabrica's reputation for employing beautiful, fun-loving female workers. Controversially, when Irish traveller Walter Starkie visited in the 1930s, he said that he had never seen 'an uglier collection of women in his life' – he was uncontroversially run out of town. The building itself was far from ugly; both grand and grandiose, the factory was the second largest building in Spain when it was originally built, but its beautifully sculptured ornate limestone facade belies its original purpose. The building is now part of the University of Seville.

Heading onwards, we sought shade from the orange trees that lined the surrounding streets. Somewhat disappointingly the oranges were green, but each year 150,000 tonnes of the fruit are harvested from the city's 40,000 trees.

Too bitter for most people's tastes, Seville oranges are generally used to make marmalade. Temporarily stopping under the shade of one tree, we looked across to the Hotel Alfonso XIII. The hotel is the grandest in Seville, and the neo-Baroque facade was both elegant and impressive. We thought about going inside to see if the interior matched the exterior, but for once we were too shy to ask. Continuing slowly onwards, we eventually arrived at our main port of call.

There is simply nothing that is shy or retiring about Seville Cathedral – the Catedral de Santa María de la Sede is the largest Gothic cathedral and the third-largest church in the world. It's a massive edifice that makes a clear statement of aim, intent and belief. 'We are here. We have conquered. We are Roman Catholic.' No expense was spared in the cathedral's construction. It was designed as a tribute to God and heaven above, but also as a triumphal monument. We decided to step inside. In a subtle attempt to emulate Catholicism, wherein the path to heaven is paved with good intentions, but often guided by profit, we instructed Tom to lie about his age and got Will to produce his student card before paying a reduced fee and entering the inner sanctum of the Gothic masterpiece.

We had to queue for quite some time before entering the cathedral. The transition from sun to shadow, from blistering heat to crisp coolness, and from the sublime to the extraordinary was nearly enough to bring on a religious conversion. The interior of the cathedral was simply awe-inspiring and it's hard to believe that such magnificence could have been accomplished without the benefit of any modern technology. Awe-inspiring today, you can only imagine just how awe-inspired people must have been when its doors first opened. The whole structure of the building would have confirmed faith and made the power and mystery of God a certain reality. Grey columns guide your eyes heavenward; the size, the scale, seem simply preposterous. When construction was first proposed, Sevillianos decided that they wanted to build a cathedral that would inspire future generations to think that they must have been mad – I think they succeeded. What's more, it's not just the size and the scale of the cathedral that's astonishing, it's the unapologetic and ostentatious display of wealth. The *retablo*, a vast Gothic altarpiece, comprising forty-five scenes from the life of Christ, is the best example of Catholic 'gilt' that I have ever seen. The altarpiece was the lifetime's work of a single craftsman, Pierre Dancart. In addition to Pierre's masterpiece, there are paintings by Goya and Murillo, a treasury full of silver and golden reliquaries, the crown of the Virgen de los Reyes and the keys of Seville. The keys were presented to Ferdinand of Castile and Leon, by the Moorish and Jewish communities on the surrender of the city in 1248. Supplicants entering the cathedral must think that they have the keys to paradise.

Apart from the keys of Seville, much of the wealth on display in the cathedral can be linked to Spain's 'Golden Age', following the discovery of the Americas. The man who paved the way for Spain's 'Golden Age' was chief discoverer Christopher Columbus. Columbus is said to be buried in the cathedral, but it's a complicated story

A great adventurer and explorer in his own lifetime, many people argue that Columbus travelled further after his death than he did while he was still alive. Columbus died in 1506, and his remains were first interred in Valladolid. Columbus had expressed a desire to be buried in the New World that he had discovered, but in 1506 there were no buildings there impressive enough to house such an important and revered corpse. In 1509, his remains were moved for the first time, to the convent at La Cartuja, near Seville. In 1537, his bones and those of his son Diego were sent from Spain to Santo Domingo. Today, Santo Domingo is the capital of the Dominican Republic. Columbus had had his wish fulfilled, he had returned to the New World. In 1795, France took over the entire island of Hispaniola, and the remains of the great explorer were moved to Havana for safekeeping. Unfortunately, the remains weren't safe for long. Spain went to war with the United States and the remains were sent back to Spain to protect them from falling into the wrong hands; namely, the Americans. Safely arriving in Spain, the remains of Christopher Columbus were finally laid to rest in Seville Cathedral – or were they?

In 1877, workers in Santo Domingo found a heavy lead box inscribed with the words 'Illustrious and distinguished male, don Cristobal Colon'. Inside the box were a set of human remains and many people now assume that these are the earthly remains of Columbus. The evidence of the inscription on the box appears to be supported by the fact that these remains show signs of advanced arthritis, an ailment from which Columbus was known to have suffered.

However, it's not that simple. Nothing usually is.

The Spanish categorically disagree with the conclusions formulated in the Dominican Republic. They have two main arguments. Firstly, DNA extracted from the bones in Seville is an extremely close match to that of Columbus's brother, Diego. Secondly, the various posthumous journeys of Columbus are well documented and are thus supported by evidence. Perhaps not unsurprisingly, the Dominican Republic dispute the Spanish counterclaims. They point out that DNA was difficult to extract and that the bones reputed to be those of Columbus do not appear to match a person of his physique or his age at death. The Dominican Republic, however, refuses to authorise its own DNA test on its own Columbus. This could be considered suspicious, but they are only a small country and they rely upon tourism. They have everything to lose and nothing to gain if their claim proves to be false.

Of course, it is just possible that both claims could be true. In 1795, half of Columbus could have been sent to Cuba, while the other half remained in Santo Domingo. Perhaps even today, Columbus straddles two continents? He might literally have a foot in both camps.

Whatever the truth of the tale, there's no denying the fact that the sarcophagus of Columbus in Seville Cathedral is held aloft by four mighty carved figures. The figures represent the four kingdoms of Aragon, Castile, Navarre and Leon.

Before the time of Columbus, the site of Seville Cathedral was occupied by a mosque. Construction of the cathedral didn't start until 153 years after the Reconquista. Fortunately, the Spanish conquest didn't result in the wholesale destruction of the Moorish city. To be fair to the Catholic monarchs of Spain, they recognised good architecture when that saw it. Just prior to victory, and just before being handed the keys of the city, the Spanish warned the Moors that if any of the great buildings of Seville were destroyed, a massacre of the innocent (and probably the not-so-innocent) would take place. On entering the largely unscathed city, the Spanish rededicated the ancient mosque to the Virgin and used it as their principal place of worship. It was only when the original Muslim mosque fell into disrepair that the cathedral was built.

Little of the former mosque now remains, but what does remain is the Giralda; a former minaret which is now the bell tower of the cathedral. The Giralda takes its name from the weathervane that tops the tower. The vane is said to symbolise the victory of the Christian faith over the Muslim Moors; it takes the shape of a female warrior with a shield in one hand and a palm in the other. Despite its Christian embellishment, the Giralda is widely proclaimed to be one of the best examples of Islamic architecture in the world.

Leaving Columbus and contention behind us, we entered the base of the Giralda. I was surprised to discover that instead of steps, a series of inclined ramps (thirty-five in all) guide the way to the top. The interior passageway is constructed from small bricks, rather than large blocks, and the passageway was designed to be just wide enough to accommodate two horsemen riding side by side. Unfortunately horseless, Tania, Will, Tom and I put one foot in front of the other as we began to tackle the 343-foot climb to the top. As we climbed, we passed interior rooms which displayed interesting artefacts from the original mosque and from a Christian church that predated the cathedral. Within the exterior walls, large apertures provided increasingly spectacular views of Seville and of the cathedral itself. The openings also provided safe places to stop and rest without blocking the path and incurring the wrath of fellow climbers.

The interior of the building was relatively cool, but we warmed up as we made our way to the bell tower. Upon reaching our goal, we hoped and prayed that the bells would remain silent; the resulting crescendo would have temporarily, if not permanently, deafened us. The climb had been hot and hard work, but the views from the top of the tower more than justified the effort involved. The whole city of Seville (apart from the Giralda) stretched out before us, a 360-degree panorama of delight.

Seville Cathedral and the Giralda whetted our appetite for further exploration, but they also kindled a desire for food and drink – it was time for '*menú del dia*'. The menu of the day is the cheapest way to eat out in Spain. You will usually be offered a starter (*primero plato*), a main meal (*segundo plato*), a dessert (*postre*) and a drink – all for somewhere between about 8 and 15 euros. Only usually served at lunchtimes, '*el menú del dia*' is a great way to feed a family and remain solvent. Choice is sometimes limited, but if you're prepared to experiment, you will not only get the best prices, but some of the best food available. Served all over Spain, '*menú del dia*' will usually be chalked up on a blackboard outside most eateries; if it isn't, you can always ask for it. '*Menú del dia*' also has the advantage of freeing up the evening for tapas.

Indulging our appetite for both food and exploration, we left the Giralda behind us and returned to street level to begin another gastronomic quest. We scanned the blackboards and printed menus outside a selection of restaurants before making our final choice.

Fully comprehending Spanish menus can sometimes be a challenge, but in response to the increasing number of English-speaking tourists visiting Andalusia each year, many restaurants now translate their menus. Far be it for me to criticise anyone else's grasp of a foreign language, but this relatively recent practice has given rise to some interesting translations. Who would really want to order 'soap of the day' (*sopa del dia*), 'drunk pork chop' (*chuleta borracha*), 'mess of ham' (*revuelto con jamón*) or 'hair in potato balls' (*bolas empanadas de carne y patata*).

Successfully avoiding hair, soap and drunk pigs, we enjoyed *salmorejo* (a delicious Andalusian version of gazpacho), followed by a tasty Iberico stew, but we were disappointed by the lack of a *postre*. We really should have read the small print (chalk) more carefully!

One thing that we are always careful about when travelling abroad is embracing local traditions and customs. One tradition that we planned to fully embrace was the siesta, a short nap taken in the afternoon. Siestas are common in countries where temperatures are high at midday and where people eat a big meal at lunchtime. Having just completed two substantial courses, we headed back to the hotel for some air-conditioned rest and relaxation.

A few hours later, and after a reviving nap, we re-emerged into the heat of the afternoon. It would have been more sensible to have kept out the heat for another hour or so, but we needed to allow sufficient time to do justice to the Alcazar.

The Alcazar of Seville, or Real Alcazar, is reputed to be one of the most beautiful palaces in Spain. The building is regarded as being one of the most outstanding examples of Mudejar architecture found anywhere in the Iberian Peninsula. Mudejar was the style developed by Moors working under Christian rule. Although the Alcazar was originally built solely by the Moors on the site of a Roman barracks, the present structure dates almost entirely from the Christian period. Pedro the Cruel created the present palace with the help of the Muslim emir of Granada, Mohammed V. Mohammed sent along an army of his best artisans and they were joined by Christian craftsman from Seville and Toledo. The result of this multi-faith workforce is a unique and beautiful blend of Iberian and Islamic art. The upper levels of the palace are still used by the Spanish royal family; it's the oldest royal palace still in use in Europe.

Entering the Alcazar via the Puerta del Leon, a striking gateway flanked by original Almohad walls, we were immediately faced with an almost impossible decision: which way should we turn? A succession of beautiful gardens, magnificent buildings and delightful courtyards opened up before our expectant eyes. Left, right or straight ahead, all options looked equally tempting. It was impossible to know which way to turn, but we tried left. We entered an exquisitely tiled and wonderfully cool building: the Sale de Justicia – the building satisfied the soul and would have gladdened the hardest of hearts. The building led us to a charming courtyard, the Patio del Yeso. The patio contained an enchanting pond, surrounded by luxuriant planting; it's one of the few remnants of the original 12th-century palace. Beautiful to see and to experience, I was lost for words. I felt physically and emotionally moved – the architects and designers had created a little piece of heaven on Earth.

Reluctant to leave such an exquisite location, we eventually tore ourselves away and continued our exploration. We walked through the Patio de la Monteria (The Hunting Courtyard), and entered the Casa de la Contratacion; it was here that Fernando and Isabel met with Columbus and other explorers of the New World. The Sala de Audiencias (Audience Hall) is hung with tapestry representations of the shields of Spanish admirals and a 16th-century *retablo* by Alejo Fernández, depicting the Virgen de los Mareantes (Virgin of the Sailors). The Virgen de los Mareantes is the earliest known painting about the discovery of the Americas.

From the Sala de Audiencias, we reached the very heart of the palace. We discovered the wonderful Patio de las Doncellas (Patio of the Maidens); it's surrounded by beautiful arches, plasterwork and tiling. The sunken garden in the centre was uncovered by archaeologists in 2004 from beneath a 16th-century marble covering. The area is alleged to commemorate the annual tribute of 100 virgins paid to the Moorish rulers by Spanish Christians. From the Patio de las Doncellas, we walked through to the Salon de Embajadores (Salon of the Ambassadors). Considered to be the most impressive room in the whole of the Alcazar, we gazed in wonder at the red, green and golden domed ceiling and the intricately patterned Mudejar tiles.

The Salon de Embajadores was truly spectacular, but I'm not sure that any one room in the Alcazar can be considered any more spectacular than any other. Everything we had seen so far had been simply stunning. The Alcazar exceeded all expectations and it has an almost otherworldly feel about it; that's probably why it has been used as a set for 'Game of Thrones'. With so many marvellous interiors, we wondered if the exterior gardens could possibly compete? The answer was a resounding yes.

The gardens were spacious, tranquil and beautiful – they contained cooling fountains, pools, water chutes, orange groves and hedgerows. Rather than just one garden, the area is a collection of many small but perfectly formed gardens. From one of these, the Jardín de las Danzas (Garden of the Dances), we followed a passageway to the Baños (Baths) of Lady María de Padilla. The baths are actually rainwater tanks, named after María de Padilla, the mistress of Peter the Cruel. The interior space was illuminated by blocks of orange and golden light and the vaulted ceiling was reflected in the water tanks. The reflected arches formed near perfect circles which gradually diminished to a vanishing point of brilliant white – the illusion was breathtaking.

The gardens were another piece of heaven on Earth, but the temperature was hellish. We hugged the shade and tried to cool ourselves under the sprinklers that brought life to the Jardin Inglés (English Garden), but it didn't really work. Still hot and now a little damp, we retreated to the interior shadows of the Palacios Gotico, but what we really needed was a bar and a drink.

Heading back towards the main cathedral square, our bar of choice turned out to be the Bodega Santa Cruz; our choice was based upon some Spanish words of wisdom. A work colleague informed me that the best bars in Spain are those that are old, run down and full of locals. With unquestionable logic, Jose Maria told me that, 'The best bars don't need to look good to get people through the door.' So far, this theory (let's call it Jose's Law) has never failed to impress.

Although the name on the wall said Bodega Santa Cruz, the bar is rather aptly known as Las Columnas; two columns framed the entrance to the dark and dingy, but quite delightful, interior. The bar was another of the basic but brilliant type. Everything looked a little old and a little tired, no airs and graces were spared by the staff, but the food, the drink and the atmosphere were second to none. We really enjoyed the *flamenquin*: slices of serrano ham wrapped in pieces of pork loin, coated with egg and breadcrumbs and then deep-fried. At the end of our all-too-brief stay, we were thrilled to find that our bill was ceremoniously chalked on the bar top.

I didn't want to leave, but the Bodega Santa Cruz was a warm-up for the evening to come – culinary foreplay for a night of gastronomic gratification. Our plan, a tapas tour of Seville.

'RELAX AND SING'

That Was Then

A disco ball sparkles in the centre of a sweaty and crowded club – I'm temporarily transfixed. Holly Johnson's voice bursts out from the speakers, accompanied by a thumping bass for a passionate race. 'Relax don't do it, when you want to go to it – Relax don't do it, when you want to come.'

Breaking out of my own personnel reverie – or drink-induced coma – I spin round on my heel and survey the scene: a 360-degree panorama of hedonistic excess. People dance, people drink, people smoke (copious amounts of tobacco and weed), people scream, people shout and people sing along – 'Relax don't do it, when you want to suck, do it.'

I have only been in Spain for thirty-six hours, but I haven't met any Andalusians who speak English, and why should they? However, despite the linguistic barriers, everyone appears to know the lyrics of all the English songs on offer. I find myself wondering just how much they really understand; Holly could well be singing about anything or everything.

Surveying the scene, I'm amazed, and for a few good reasons. Firstly, I'm amazed by the fact that I have a 360-degree panorama; I'm not tall, just 5ft10, but in post-Franco Spain, where people have been rationed and frequently starved, I'm the tallest person in the room. Secondly, I'm amazed because I'm listening to songs from British bands; I thought it was all going to be Julio Iglesias and 'Europop'. Thirdly, I'm amazed because it's three in the morning and the club doesn't shut until six.

Leaving Ariana to dance, I search for a table. It's been another long day and the wine has definitely kicked in. Sitting and surveying the scene, and trying to stop the scene from spinning, I hear the first English words spoken by anyone apart from Ariana since my arrival. Marit introduces herself over a drink; we chat, or more accurately shout as Holly keeps singing – 'Live those dreams – Scheme those schemes.'

I discover that Marit is from Norway, and 'Relax' reaches its climax – 'Gotta hit me, (hit me) hit me with those laser beams'.

Possibly taking her cue from the song, Marit asks me if I want to come back

to hers. 'I'm with my girlfriend,' I reply. 'She can come as well,' Marit suggests. I look confused and an uncertain emotion forces an uncertain smile. Marit picks up on my expression. 'Three together. How you know you not like it, if you don't try it?'

She has a point, but she leaves alone.

THIS IS NOW

Bats shine as they flutter into and out of the Giralda bell tower, caught in the spotlights that illuminate the city – I'm temporarily transfixed. Ed Sheeran's voice breaks out from the bar-top hi-fi, serenading the scene – 'It's late in the evening, glass on the side.'

Breaking out of my own personnel reverie, or state of near-perfect contentment, I spin round and survey the scene: a 360-degree panorama of calm delight. Buildings gleam, the moon shines, shadows shimmy, people talk, people drink and I sing along – 'I've been sat with you, for most of the night, ignoring everybody here, we wish they would disappear.'

I have only been in Spain for thirty-six hours, but I already feel totally at ease and totally content. Tania and I have returned to our rooftop refuge, the boys are in bed and our tapas tour has been a great success.

Surveying the scene, I'm amazed, and for a few good reasons. Firstly, I'm amazed by the fact that I'm drinking on a rooftop bar overlooking the wondrous city of Seville, for the second night in a row. Secondly, I'm amazed because I feel fantastic and pretty much our whole holiday still stretches out before us. Thirdly, I'm amazed because I didn't think I liked Ed Sheeran, but I do.

Leaving the metropolitan views to themselves, I sit down at a table. It's been another long day and the drink is beginning to kick in. Sitting and surveying the scene, I'm reminded of how lucky I am to be here. It's all too easy to moan and complain, but sometimes life can be perfect – live those dreams.

I chat to Tania, as Ed sings – 'I need you darling, come on set the tone, if you feel you're falling, won't you let me know.'

Tania hands me a glass of something blue – I pull a face and an uncertain emotion forces an uncertain smile. 'How do you know you don't like it, if you don't try it?'

Tania has a point, but I buy a beer.

CORDOBA

THIS IS NOW

After a long breakfast and a lazy morning, we left Seville and headed off towards Cordoba. We reached the outskirts of the city in the heat of the early afternoon, but with a sense of déjà vu we immediately began to regret our decision to stay in the heart of the ancient city – forewarned is not always forearmed!

Cordoba had recently undergone some major road and traffic reconfiguration; our satellite navigation system and the majority of road signs were now obsolete. We knew that reaching our hotel was going to be problematic, but the Don Paula Hotel had come up with an interesting solution – the hotel had posted an online YouTube clip. Shot from the front of a car and filmed in real time, the clip demonstrated the appropriate line of approach. What could possibly go wrong? We downloaded the clip and Tania watched it on her iPad as we entered the inner city. Tania relayed instructions, but it wasn't a straightforward business. Tania played the clip and instructed me to turn right, but we had already driven past the requisite right turn. Tania pressed pause and rewound the clip as I reversed the car, causing general mayhem in the process. Tania couldn't find where we had got to in the clip, so I parked as Tania frantically searched for the right position, but the clip kept buffering and tempers began to fray. Tania selected play again, so I headed off, but then we lost our connection with both 3G and reality and I had to brake hard. Play, drive, pause, stop, rewind, reverse – it was a frustrating and hazardous process.

After what seemed like an eternity and without really knowing how we had achieved it, we breathed a sigh of relief as we arrived at a small courtyard outside the Don Paula Hotel. With the help of the YouTube clip, locating the hotel had been challenging (to say the least), without the clip it would have been impossible. The hotel, however, was worth the effort. Family run, the welcome could not have been friendlier. We were offered a drink and given some tips on the sights and timings of visits while our car was whisked away to a location unknown and uncared about. I was delighted that we had had the foresight to prepay for valet parking. The rooms were perfect with complimentary fruit and water, comfortable beds, beautiful bathrooms and air conditioning. The

temptation to just relax and chill out was almost overwhelming, but we decided to venture out straight away as we only had one night in which to explore the city.

Cordoba is packed full of delights. The city was the capital of Hispania Baetica during the days of the Roman Empire, and then it became the Islamic capital of most of the Iberian Peninsula. Today, Cordoba is moderately sized, but it is believed that in the 10th century it was the most populous and one of the most advanced cities in the world. The old town (another UNESCO World Heritage Site) contains numerous reminders of Cordoba's glorious past.

Our hotel was located in the old Jewish quarter, so we were well situated, right in the heart of the ancient city. We walked from the hotel towards the Mezquita (The Great Mosque/Cathedral of Cordoba). Strolling through delightfully shaded alleyways and streets, we remembered 'Jose's Law' and looked out for suitable places to eat for later in the day.

Following an irregular path through the labyrinthine streets, we eventually emerged into a courtyard surrounding the Mezquita – El Patio de los Naranjos. The courtyard was exquisite. Planted with orange trees and palms and watered by irrigation channels, it was here that the faithful cleansed themselves before prayer. Although it has officially been a Christian site for almost nine centuries, the Mezquita's Muslim identity was inescapable.

Entrance to 'El Patio de los Naranjos' was free of charge, and if we had arrived earlier in the day and attended a morning service, entry to the Mezquita would have been free as well – afternoon visits are by card or cash. I dusted off my wallet, headed over to the ticket booth and joined a queue. Now, I'm not usually one for cultural stereotyping, but it's my experience that the French don't like queuing. Pushing in front of us and several others, a large French family forced their way to the front of the queue and then proceeded to ask about a million questions without having the wherewithal or common decency to get a move on and just buy a ticket. And what did the rest of us do? Well, nothing. We tutted, we moaned, we gave each other sympathetic looks, but the French family got their way. *'Liberté, égalité, fraternité'* – liberty to do what you want, without much equality or fraternity.

After a longer period of time than could have accurately been predicted, we purchased our tickets and gained entrance to the Mezquita. We stepped through the Puerta del Perdon, and I stopped dead in my tracks. Faced by row upon row upon row of beautiful variegated columns and arches, all I could do was stand and stare. I wasn't alone – just about every visitor appeared to be experiencing the same emotion; we were all stunned into silence and immobility by the sheer beauty of the spectacle. It would be impossible to overemphasise the impact of Cordoba's great mosque. It is a mesmerising vision of wonder and delight – a peaceful haven of pure perfection.

Turning on the spot and looking in every direction, my sense of wonder never ceased. The terracotta and white-striped arches and columns were constructed to evoke a forest of delicate date palms – it's certainly a forest of delight. The aim of the design was to induce an expansive, meditative state for prayer – the aim was clearly achieved.

The symmetry is stunning; geometrically precise, a mathematician's dream. However, the columns, which are recycled from Roman, Visigoth and other sources, are actually all different sizes. The larger columns have been sunk into the ground and the smaller columns have been raised up to create an illusion of uniformity. In order to further this illusion, a second tier of arches was added to the first – a fortunate addition which adds to the unique elegance of the interior.

Defying precedents, the Mezquita's architectural importance and uniqueness lie in the fact that, structurally speaking, it was a revolutionary design. The Dome of the Rock in Jerusalem and the Great Mosque in Damascus both had vertical, nave-like designs, but the Mezquita's aim was to create an infinitely spacious, democratically horizontal and simple area where the spirit would be free to roam and communicate easily with God.

The Mezquita was not the first religious structure to be built on the site. After escaping to Iberia and taking over Cordoba, the exiled Umayyad prince Abd al-Rahman bought the land from the Christians, who had built a Visigothic church on top of a former Roman temple. Initially, Abd al-Rahman purchased only half of the church, which he divided with a partition so that it could serve the needs of both the Christian and Muslim communities; an enlightened approach in a European Dark Age. However, the rapid growth of the Muslim community soon meant that the space was too small, and in AD 784 he bought the other half to erect a new mosque.

Initial construction began in AD 786, and the mosque was completed within the same year; an impressive achievement. The mosque became an important pilgrimage site – at one time it held an original copy of the Koran and an arm bone of the prophet Mohammed. For the two centuries after its initial construction, the mosque was extended and altered. A new minaret was completed in the 9th century and outer aisles and the orange tree courtyard were also added, but the highlight of the mosque has to be the 10th-century Mihrab. This octagonal chamber points towards Mecca and was the sacred focal point for prayer. No expense or expertise was spared in its construction. Emperor Nicephoras sent artisans from Constantinople to help create some of the finest mosaics in existence. The Christian emperor sent the Muslim caliph not only artisans, but also a gift of 1600kg of gold mosaic cubes. The shimmering cubes, shaped into flower motifs and inscriptions from the Koran, decorate and radiate to this day.

Since its original construction, the Mezquita has undergone some minor, and one fairly major, alterations. Famously, or perhaps infamously, Emperor Carlos V decided to construct a Christian cathedral right in the centre of the mosque. Overriding the wishes of the local people, including the mayor, Carlos commissioned the construction, but he soon regretted his decision. In 1523, sixty of the original 1,013 columns were removed from the heart of the mosque to make way for the cathedral. Upon beholding the completion of the work, Carlos is quoted as saying the following – 'You have built what you or others might have built anywhere, but you have destroyed something that was unique in the world.'

I had presumed that the cathedral would be defined by walls – a separate super-structure within the mosque itself. However, the cathedral is an open plan design. One minute you are gazing at rows of columns and arches, and the next minute the roof rises and you are in a lavish, highly decorated and ostentatious Roman Catholic cathedral. Most people agree with Carlos and think that the design is a travesty, but I think that the unique mixture of Christian and Moorish architecture and Christian and Islamic faith, which gives rise to a real sense of east meets west, has created a whole that is even more stunning than its parts. The juxtaposition of Christianity and Islam, and the practice of religious one-upmanship, whereby one religion has attempted to outdo the other, has resulted in a unique and incredibly building. Put simply, the Mezquita is the most impressive and the most evocative building that I have ever visited.

Once upon a time the Mezquita was flooded by the light from nineteen open doorways, but today only one door remains open. In the dim half-light of the interior I was flooded by emotion. I stood and stared, I walked around enthralled and engaged, I wondered, I dreamed and I could almost have cried. I have never visited anywhere else that has made me feel so impassioned – it was almost a spiritual experience.

After a longer period of time than could have accurately been prophesied, we reluctantly left the cool confines of the Mezquita and headed towards the

Guadalquivir River. We walked across 'El Puente Romano' (the Roman Bridge) in blistering conditions – the sun was high in the sky; the heat was intense and shade was unfortunately absent. Although it's called the Roman Bridge, it's unlikely that much of the original structure remains; possibly only the foundations. The present structure is a medieval reconstruction and sixteen glorious Moorish arches now span the river. Halfway across the bridge we stopped at a statue of St Raphael. Candles had been lit at the base of the statue, which rather aptly depicts an archangel revered by Christians and Muslims alike. I felt a certain amount of reverence for the bridge, it's a wonderful piece of architecture and it offers excellent views of the river and the old city, but we thought that if we stayed out in the heat for much longer we would melt, so we headed back to our hotel. Before heading to Spain, we had told a Spanish friend that we planned to visit Cordoba in the summer. 'You are going to hell,' he informed us. If he was referring to the weather, he had a point.

After a cool air-conditioned siesta, early evening saw us heading out once again, our destination the Bodega Taberna Rafae. We had spotted the taberna earlier in the day and it appeared to fill all of Jose's requirements – it was old, small, family run, cheap and full of locals. Fortunately, our choice proved to be a wise one. The food was traditional, the portions were generous (more *raciones* rather than tapas) and the waiters were very friendly and very helpful. After a quick family confab, we decided that each of us would order two portions of tapas and then we would share all the food between us, but we split the order, ordering four portions of food at two different times. It's a good idea to split a tapas order, for two reasons: firstly, to ensure that the food is always hot; and secondly, to ensure that you don't order too much food. Ordering in turn, we ended up trying to out-compete each other in terms of the adventurousness of the dishes that we chose – a case of culinary one-upmanship that saw us eating Cordoban-style tripe, bull's tail and octopus, as well as some mystery dishes that we couldn't translate. The one thing that all the dishes had in common (apart from the tripe) was that they were all delicious, as was the wine that Tania and I used to aid digestion.

Digestion was also aided by the Spanish attitude to food and drink. In Spain, food and drink are seen as pleasures to be enjoyed and appreciated and mealtimes are a real occasion. Sometimes fast food is the answer to our immediate needs, but how preferable it is to be able to take your time and fully appreciate each morsel of food, each mouthful of drink and each relaxing second of a leisurely-consumed meal. Nourishment for the body and the soul. Taking our time, the boys followed their tapas with a *postre* of *natillas* – a custard made from milk and eggs – while Tania and I sampled some *manzanilla* – a local fino sherry, dry, pale and slightly salty.

We took so much time over our meal that by the time we had finished, night had fallen. Leaving Bodega Taberna Rafae, we welcomed the relative coolness of the evening and headed back towards the river and the Roman Bridge, via the Alcazar de los Reyes Cristianos (Alcazar of the Christian Monarchs).

Spotlights illuminated the towers and great walls of the palace-cum-fortress. Originally built in the 8th century as a caliphate residence, the area was rebuilt and reconfigured by Alfonso XI in the 14th century. It was in the Alcazar de los Reyes Cristianos that Ferdinand and Isabella first met Columbus, who explained his somewhat errant plan to find a westbound sea route to India. It was also here that the Inquisition made its headquarters, converting many of the buildings, including the Arab baths, into torture and interrogation chambers – I bet no one expected that! The Alcazar was closed when we walked past, but we could see into some of magnificent gardens – floodlit fountains, orange trees, flowers and topiary paid homage to the Alcazar's Moorish past.

Continuing onwards, we walked past the Caballerizas Reales de Cordoba. The riding stables date from 1570, and were launched to create a pure Spanish thoroughbred, the Andalusian horse. The stables looked magnificent, but we didn't enter. The stables weren't closed, but our wallets were. We didn't see a show, but we did see several of the famous Spanish horses and carriages entering the arena. Apparently, it's free to enter the stables and see the horses during the day.

Thinking that we might return in the morning, but knowing that we probably wouldn't, we left the stables and ended up walking along the right bank of the Guadalquivir River, gazing at the Roman Bridge. Lights placed under each of the sixteen arches illuminated the bridge and enveloped it in shades of yellow, white and gold. The bridge looked even more spectacular by night than it had by day. We joined other late night promenaders and headed across the bridge to the Calahorra Tower. The Almohads built the tower to protect the bridge, but it now protects Andalusian heritage; the tower contains a small museum which depicts life in 10th-century Cordoba. Dropping down from the tower to the river, we were buzzed by bats which feasted on swarms of insects attracted by the bright lights. Tania was less than happy, but the boys and I were amazed, so we decided to venture into the middle of the feeding frenzy. Sounding like a poor man's David Attenborough, I spoke to the boys in hushed tones – 'Bats use their own form of sonar to navigate and consequently they never crash into anything.' Looking like a poor man's David Attenborough, a bat flew straight into my face.

That Was Then

'What the hell was that?' I shrieked. Something had brushed against the side of my face. 'Keep quiet, it's only a bat,' said Ariana.

I was already feeling slightly agitated, but my close encounter with a flying mammal made the situation even worse. Looking up into the night sky, I could see several bats silhouetted by a crescent moon.

'Who's going to hear us?' I said. 'No one else is going to be stupid enough to break into the Alhambra.'

'You'd be surprised,' said Ariana. 'Anyway, we're not breaking in, it's free to visit. We're just visiting out of hours.'

Earlier that evening, one of Ariana's Spanish friends had suggested that a night-time visit to the Alhambra, the jewel in Granada's crown, was a must for any visitor. Later in the evening, after consuming numerous glasses of wine, the idea seemed like a good one.

Pushing through a break in an exterior fence, armed with a bottle of red, some bread and some cheese, we entered the gardens. Navigating by faint moonlight, an underpowered torch and touch, we began to explore the historic site.

In early 1984, the Alhambra was yet to become a UNESCO World Heritage Site. The buildings and gardens were important for tourism, but much of the complex was in need of restoration and security was lax.

We wandered into and out of buildings and rooms, catching glimpses of wonderful mosaics, ponds, pools and courtyards. We experienced the peace, the quiet, the isolation and the illicit joy of exploring somewhere that we really shouldn't have been. The night was still, but the silence was occasionally broken by odd sounds, magnified by contrast – another bat, a leaf rustling in a rare breeze, the echo of our footsteps and the echo of the past. The air was fresh and the atmosphere was intoxicating – we traced patterns with our fingertips. Our senses worked overtime as we looked, heard, smelt, tasted and touched a present that recalled the past. We played at being caliphs and kings, sultans and queens, as silhouettes and shadows evoked images of ancient lives.

For one night only this was our domain, or was it?

Hearing other voices, I thought we had been discovered. Envisaging a further encounter with the Guardia Civil, I froze. It soon became apparent, however, that we weren't the only trespassers on site – our kingdom was not our own, but our legitimacy was not being contested. Wandering off in search of solitude, we met other night-time interlopers, including a group of half a dozen or so teenagers who had lit a fire in one of the ancient buildings.

Peace destroyed, solitude invaded and the moment gone. We fled the past, but new memories had been created and the future appeared to be alive with possibilities.

THIS IS NOW

Heading back from the Roman Bridge, we dropped into the Salon de Te for a nightcap. The traditional tea house was alive with possibilities – over fifty different types of tea, to be less than exact. Offering a nice change of pace from the often-frantic tapas bars, we sat back and relaxed in the charming building. Low chairs surrounded a fountain in an open courtyard; flowers, fruit, hookahs, murmuring water, enveloping aromas and Moroccan furnishings evoked a real sense of North Africa, as did the heat. Loose leaf tea was served in intricately patterned coloured glasses and silver teapots. T'ien Yiheng said that 'Tea is drunk to forget the din of the world', and Orwell famously stated that 'Tea is one of the main stays of civilisation' – agreeing with both writers, we had a civilised chat in the peaceful and calm surroundings, forgetting all but each other and the here and now. Family is not an important thing, it's everything.

'Yo te quiero infinito, yo te acuerda, oh mi corazón.'

NOWHERE FAST

That Was Then

Peeling the skin back from my eyes, I attempt to rise, but someone has placed a lead weight in my head and I crash back down to my pillow. The room spins, or is it me. My head bangs with a discordant rhythm – a thumping bass for a disaffected face. My mouth is dry; thirst is an all-consuming desire, but still my head won't rise. I cry out, thinking that I can vocally expel my demons, but the demons remain and I groan in vain. I twist and turn in an attempt to find a position that eases my pain, but nothing works. I smother my head with my pillow, blocking out background noise, but my head still beats and heat eventually forces me out from under cover. 'After a count of ten,' I promise myself. 'One, two, three, four' – my count gets slower as my decimal dawn approaches. 'Let's make that twenty,' I muse, promises are meant to be broken. I open my right eye and take a look around. Blurred vision reveals a hazy disaster zone. I open my left eye, firmly closing my right. Clothes are strewn across the tiled floor and empty bottles compete for space. I open both eyes simultaneously – it's a mistake that I soon regret and quickly rectify. Blinded by brightness, I wonder if I'll ever see again, and I promise myself that I will never drink again. Every action has a reaction and pleasure is often followed by pain – I shouldn't have listened to my id. Immediate gratification was bound to lead to dissatisfaction – the pleasure principal strikes again. Groaning involuntarily, I have the sudden feeling that if it isn't now, it's never – I try to sit up again. I succeed in stages, like a slow-motion, stop-motion character. Today is going to be a long day, but at least I'm moving.

THIS IS NOW

Today always had the potential to be a long day, but when we woke in the morning we had no idea quite how long and stressful a day it was going to be. Waking after a restful night's sleep filled with memories of our first day in Cordoba, we decided to briefly wander the ancient city's wondrous streets for

one last time before heading off towards Ronda. Yesterday's exploration hadn't allowed us time to visit one of Cordoba's most famous and most photographed tourist spots – the Calle de las Flores. Picturesque yet crowded, even in the early morning, we were impressed by the pink, purple and red geraniums in their terracotta pots which adorned the whitewashed houses on either side of the narrow-cobbled street. Standing in a tiny square at the northern end of the botanical bonanza, we gazed at a perfectly framed view of the Mezquita's tower framed by the flower-covered white walls, our view only slightly compromised by a large group of self-serving, selfie-taking tourists. I hesitate to sound like a grumpy old man (although Tania might say that's it's a common enough occurrence), but why not just look at the view and enjoy the moment? Why spend so much time preening, posing and posting, rather than just living and looking?

Interrupting carefully constructed self-portraits and dodging 'selfie sticks', we walked back down through the alley and then headed for a last look at the Patio de los Naranjos and the outer walls of the Mezquita, before enjoying a tasty breakfast of *tostada con tomate* and cafe con leche. My culinary enjoyment, however, was slightly diminished by anticipated thoughts of drama, which resulted in anguish as I contemplated trying to drive out of the heart of Cordoba. Could we play the hotel's YouTube clip in reverse? Could I get Tania to drive? Would we ever make it out of this city alive?

Anguish was fortunately soon extinguished. How could I have doubted the Don Paula Hotel's complete commitment to customer service? Sensing my apprehension as he returned my car from its overnight lodgings, our friendly proprietor leapt onto his motorbike and said, 'Follow me.' Driving at breakneck speed, whilst twisting and turning through narrow streets and driving through what appeared to be pedestrianised plazas, our gallant proprietor turned motorcycle outrider successfully guided us out of the city. Without such assistance, I truly believe that we would still be in Cordoba, and while I imagine that being trapped in Cordoba is a delight (we all regretted not staying longer), it would certainly have curtailed our subsequent travels and experiences.

Our destination was a holiday home, booked through 'Owners Direct' and located within striking distance of Ronda. But, rather than head directly for our journey's end, we decided on a detour to visit a Roman cemetery. Now, this was not just any cemetery – according to the guidebooks it is one of the most important in Spain. Lying on a low hill on the outskirts of Carmona, the Necropolois Romana houses more than 900 family tombs dating from the 2nd century BC to the 4th century AD. Entry is free and we had the place to ourselves – if you don't count the ghosts of Romans past. Visitors are given almost total access to the site, with no real supervision. We climbed down rickety ladders into some of the tombs. One of the larger ones, the Tumbe del Elefante, complete with a stone elephant, was very elaborate. Apparently, the tombs were the focus for great ceremony and celebration, before and after burial. Apart from the burial chambers, the remains of baths, pantries and banquet tables can also be seen. The largest tomb felt more like a temple and included side chambers and servant's vaults. The whole place was wonderfully evocative, but scorchingly hot. A few cypress trees provided some shade, but did little to protect us from the burning sun. Hot, sweaty and thirsty, I felt something brush against the side of my face. Flapping away a hornet, I was stung by way of response. Hot, sweaty, thirsty and now in pain, I was beginning to envy the dead – it was time to move on.

Almost immediately after picking up our hire car from Malaga airport, I had some misgivings, and a portentous feeling dominated all thoughts of driving and motoring. I'm by no means a mechanical maestro, but the car just didn't seem right. The car looked okay, but the class was not as advertised: the air conditioning functioned, but half-heartedly; the gears shifted, but the bite was high. Ever since our arrival in Seville, I had been meaning to contact the hire company and arrange to change our Nissan Note for a more noteworthy vehicle, but I had put off the phone call. My latest plan was to contact 'Auto Navarro' when we reached our holiday home. Unfortunately, this decision was slightly presumptuous.

One minute we were happily driving along a dual carriageway – the discomfort resulting from my painful encounter with a hornet was fading, I was cooling down (despite the faulty air conditioning) and my thirst had been quenched – but then disaster struck. Changing gear to adapt to a change in gradient, the car refused to comply. Stuck in the wrong gear, the car spluttered and died as we pulled over onto the hard shoulder. Miles from anywhere, we left the car and sat by the side of the road. It was now midday, the sun was high in the sky, there was no shade, no sanctuary and no immediate hope of assistance. Why do I always put things off? Frantic phone calls ensued.

After numerous, increasingly heated conversations, we managed to persuade the hire company to face up to their responsibilities and provide us with a taxi so that we could complete our journey. They also agreed to have a new hire car waiting for us at our next destination. Once agreed, we were told that help would be with us within the next ten minutes, but as each ten-minute term expired and another was promised and then not met, our faith began to wane. Ten minutes became twenty, twenty minutes became half an hour, and half an hour extended to one hour and then two. Conditions were uncomfortable to say the least. We attempted to be creative with suitcases, beach towels and umbrellas, but it was impossible to block out the sun. We smeared ourselves with sun cream and tried to be patient, but the heat was unbearable; we were running out of water and our location only served to emphasise our isolation and potential vulnerability. Stories of modern-day highway robbers filled our vivid imaginations as the moments and minutes merged. Occasionally a breakdown truck would be spotted and our hopes were raised, but they all drove by, apart from one which tried to tow our car away without any authority or jurisdiction. The day dragged by slowly and we began to worry that we wouldn't be in time to meet the owners who would provide the keys for our holiday home. I tried to read to pass the time, I observed ants as they scurried over the parched earth, I thought about all the times when I'm too busy to think and tried to appreciate the enforced inactivity, but waiting for anything makes time slow down and patience was soon in short supply.

It transpired that the hire company were reluctant to leave the car unaccompanied by the side of the road, so they wouldn't pick us up before they could arrange to pick the car up. We were reluctant to have the car picked up before we were picked up, so it all became a bit of a stalemate until the hire company, the taxi company and the breakdown company managed to arrange a coordinated response.

Not for the first time, I gazed back down the road from where we had driven. Hope filled my emotions rather than expectation, but emerging from the heat haze, like Omar Sharif in *Lawrence of Arabia*, and slowly materialising, I saw a breakdown truck heading towards us and thankfully it began to indicate its intention to stop. Shortly afterwards, a taxi followed and made its own similar intentions clear. Help was at hand.

I don't think I have ever been more grateful to see a taxi, not even when tired, cold and emotional at three in the morning one New Year's Eve, but that's another story. We quickly transferred all our possessions into the cool air-conditioned confines of the taxi and headed south. Our enjoyment of the journey was magnified by contrast; it was a long and circuitous trip, but we were cool and comfortable and for the most part calm. I chatted to the driver in a mixture of broken Spanish and English as we journeyed ever further. The driver seemed happy to be out of his normal routine, until, that is, we began climbing the narrow and sometimes near vertical roads in the Serrania de Ronda. I don't think town and city driving had prepared our driver for the vertiginous slopes and death-defying drops that led towards Ronda, Cartijima and our isolated casa, perched on its own precipice. As the roads narrowed and the drops steepened our taxi driver gripped the wheel tightly, this really was becoming a white-knuckle ride. '*Joder*,' he chanted, over and over again, as he stared into the abyss and thought that the drop was getting ready to welcome him. Occasionally, from my angle, it looked like half the taxi was in midair, but then stone and tarmac would fill the scene. My mind went back to 1984 and my coach trip to Granada, but despite the disconcerting ramblings of the driver and apart from a slight concern that I would have to drive these very roads if we were ever going to leave our holiday home, I was happy to be moving.

MI CASA

That Was Then

Thankful to have re-joined the living, I felt weary, but I decided to explore the flat.

In Spain, flats or apartments are far more common than in the UK. In actual fact, the Spanish are some of the world's most pre-eminent apartment-dwellers. In 2012, roughly 65 per cent of the population lived in apartment buildings, much higher than the euro-area average of 46 per cent and the UK rate of 14.5 per cent. This predilection for high-rise living can partly be explained by Spain's tumultuous history. In Spain, and to a slightly lesser extent across most of mainland Europe, internal struggles and international wars continued into modern times and created an atmosphere of fear and uncertainty in rural areas. Consequently, many people felt safer living within city walls. As trouble roamed outside the city gates, so a style and habit of communal, cramped living developed. In the UK, many people safely abandoned cities at an early stage in history and spread out on a horizontal plane into the countryside, whereas the Spanish developed a vertical urban lifestyle. This high-rise style

was compounded by Franco, who restricted the growth of cities to protect agricultural land.

My exploration initially arose out of necessity – I needed to find the toilet and I needed to find some painkillers, both needs were pressing. The flat was temporarily empty, Ariana had left for the university and I had yet to meet her flatmate. The time for exploration was ripe. The flat was located a short bus ride away from the centre of Granada. Part of a modern five-storey block, we were on the fourth floor, with shops on the entrance level. One of the first things I noticed when I arrived was a unique and strong smell of Spanish bleach, which not only pervaded the outside of the building, but the inside as well. For the Spanish, cleanliness is definitely next to godliness, and in 1984, godliness was still pretty high on the agenda. The smell of bleach and disinfectant was everywhere, and the smell stayed with you. I thought I was going to be sick.

Heading towards the bathroom, I entered a cupboard by mistake before finding the right door. Downing some painkillers and drinking copious amounts of water, my head slowly began to clear and I continued on my road to recovery – I hoped this particular road wasn't going to be a dead end.

Feeling better by the second, but worried that this might just be a false dawn, I started to explore in earnest. The flat was small, space was at a premium, but it was neat and tidy (apart from our room) and well equipped. Two bedrooms, a living room, a kitchen, the bathroom and a separate toilet led off from an entrance hall. I had already discovered the bathroom; the kitchen was next. I poked around in the cupboards and the fridge, but even if I had fancied something to eat, the cupboards were bare. The living room contained a small TV, a sofa, a table, some books, a guitar and what looked like a dressing-up box, but it turned out to be the apartment owner's spare clothes and appeared to include a dead fox – it was actually a stole, but it looked healthier than me. Throwing open the living room window, a small balcony was revealed. I presumed that fresh air would aid recovery. Optimistically selecting a Hemingway, I gazed over suburban rooftops and listened to the mosquito-like buzz of scooters and the chiming of church bells, before collapsing into a foetal position and grabbing my head. My recovery had indeed been a false dawn and I wondered for whom the bells tolled.

THIS IS NOW

As soon we pulled onto the dirt track driveway, things began to come together. Our host awaited us with a set of keys, a new hire car was parked further along the driveway, the taxi driver smiled with visible relief and Casa Mesto looked simply stunning.

Casa Mesto occupied a small area of flat land, a level terrace, bordered by steep slopes above and below. The traditional white villa, crowned with terracotta tiles, sat on a ledge amidst a wonderland of extraordinary rock formations. Officially called *los Riscos*, limestone outcrops have been sculptured by the wind and the rain to produce a quite amazing landscape. Steep slopes fell down in front of the level situation of the house to the valley below. The hillsides were heavily forested with dwarf oaks, stunted by the barren soil, dry rock and harsh conditions. Rising on the opposite side of the valley, the steep slopes were again mostly forested, but occasional glimpses of red soil and isolated farms broke through the sylvan beauty of the area. In the far distance a range of high, angular, peaked mountains, the Sierra Bermeja, provided a perfect backdrop. The barren, red-hued heights of the Sierra Bermeja rise to about 1,000 metres, and separate the Serrania de Ronda from the Mediterranean coast. To the south-east, the village of Pujerra nestled on another level platform. The *pueblo blanco* glistened in the sun – at night the same houses, illuminated by light, appeared to float in the air and resembled an undiscovered constellation.

Tearing ourselves away from the view, we left our taxi driver talking to his controller (I think he was trying to find a way home that didn't involve death-defying drops) and followed the owner of the house as he guided us inside Casa Mesto. The entrance was guarded by a massive solid oak door, further strengthened with iron bolts, the door also featured a spyhole protected with an iron grille. The entrance hall, complete with a Moroccan-styled ceiling, led to an ornate L-shaped hall. The house incorporated three bedrooms, all of which were painted white with terracotta floor tiles and beautifully furnished with antique wooden dressers and wardrobes. The rooms were finished off with colourful wall hangings and tasteful knick-knacks. Our bedroom provided a glorious mountain view and just outside the window was a tempting fig tree, laden with fruit. The lounge included a small TV (that we never used), an open fireplace (which we didn't need to use) and more antique furniture (some of which we were afraid to use). All objects were illuminated by the light from a huge bronze chandelier.

Stepping back outside the house, a shaded patio with a bamboo slatted roof, raised on ancient beams and dotted with geraniums in blue pots, looked like the perfect spot to enjoy a late lingering breakfast or a cool sleepy supper. A path led from the patio up to a roof terrace which basically sat above the kitchen. Complete with its own crenelated walls, it looked like it would offer a last line of defence if ever the need arose. Already enraptured by what we had seen, we walked back down past the patio and discovered an infinity pool, which contained the most exquisitely blue water I think I have ever seen. The outer edge of the pool adjoined a precipitous drop and was slightly lower than the other three sides; water lapped deliciously over the edge. Behind the pool, the garden ended by a boundary fence; here we discovered five free-range goats, who would eventually pick up the courage to eat out of our hands. Between the patio and the pool, a manicured lawn heralded the promise of blissful afternoons of reading and relaxation. Above the lawn, a front terrace ran along the entire length of the property – southward facing, it looked like the perfect sun trap.

No words were required. We looked at each other and smiled.

A DAY IN THE LIFE

THIS IS NOW

Casa Mesto was idyllic, a tranquil slice of paradise.

After the excitement of Seville and Cordoba, and the stress of travelling, we were ready for a few days of doing nothing much at all. Apart from a brief excursion to the outskirts of Ronda to gather some provisions, we gave in to a life of leisure and pleasure as we basked in our surroundings. Minutes and moments merged as we drank, ate, slept, talked, swam, sunbathed, read and relaxed. Time began to lose meaning as the days developed their own rhythm.

Our day usually started shortly after the break of dawn. I would like to be able to describe the sunrise, but we never managed to wake up in time. I never made it up before 7:30, and by then the sun had already risen. Falling out of bed, grabbing a shower and brewing a coffee, I ventured out into the cool of morning, hoping to catch sight of a fox who allegedly drank each morning from the swimming pool. Although mostly quiet and peaceful, each period of the day had its own acoustic accompaniment. Dogs were the first to greet the dawn as they barked and incited

each other to an ever more frantic frenzy, born of impatience as they demanded their breakfasts. We breakfasted on the shaded patio and planned the day ahead – it never took too much planning. Temperatures were cool until about 10:00 a.m., but then the sun rose high and bathed all but a few shaded areas in bright sunshine and enveloped all in an intense heat. The cicadas began to chirp as we shifted between pool and patio, between sun and shade. Goats bleated and bells tinkled as animals grazed just out of sight. Occasionally the passage of a car, and sometimes the sharp retort of gunfire, echoed across the hillsides. The hottest part of the day followed, between 2:30 and 4:30 in the afternoon; hiding from the sun, we eat tapas under our bamboo screen. After lunch we alternated between reading, sunbathing, swimming and resting as the day slowly and imperceptibly cooled and evening slowly approached. Wine opened, we drank and ate food inspired by our location as we soaked up the views serenaded by birdsong and the gentle hum of insects. Swifts and swallows, followed by the arrival of bats, announced dusk, which always fell between 9:00 and 10:00 p.m. We toasted the night as a bright moon rose in the sky and shadows slowly climbed up the valley and over Pujerra. A moonlight swim in the now cool water of the pool was followed by a warming shower, a final drink before bed and a false promise to be up before the next dawn.

That Was Then

Thankfully, not all days were the same, but a certain pattern and rhythm did begin to emerge. Heading back to bed, I slept for another couple of hours, before rising to face the day for a second time. I was awoken by the cry of a neighbour's baby, but it was hardly an unsociable hour, so I couldn't really complain. Feeling far more human than I had any right to expect, I showered, dressed and headed out for a coffee. A pneumatic drill made me grimace, but a small bar situated on the ground floor of our apartment provided a lifesaving beverage for just a few pesetas. Drinking slowly, I attempted to read a local newspaper, but soon settled for watching the news on a large television, which blasted out at full volume to anyone who cared to listen. I cared to listen, but I couldn't understand much of what was being said. I could only pick out a few words and that wasn't really enough to be able find out what was going on in the world. My Spanish may well have been terrible, but the coffee was excellent. Feeling marginally better, I thought I might try something to eat. I ordered churros (pieces of fried and sugared dough) and dipped them in my coffee. I immediately felt much better – a sugar rush was obviously what was required. I lingered over my coffee and churros for quite some time, but nobody cared. There were only a few people in the bar and I had already discovered that lingering over food and drink is part and parcel of being Spanish. I communicated, rather than chatted with the waiter and an elderly gentleman who sat close by – it's amazing just how much you can convey with a couple of words and sign language. In 1984, English people were a bit of a rarity in Granada, and most people I met were interested and intrigued about my status and nationality. It became apparent that my new Spanish friends thought that there were only two types of English people: football hooligans and bowler-hatted gents carrying black umbrellas. Hopefully, as I was without either hat, umbrella or tattoo, I encouraged them to reassess their preconceptions.

Eventually running out of things I could mime, I wished all a friendly *adiós* and headed out for a short wander around the local shops. The streets were fairly full and people queued at a range of different stores. Butchers, bakers, fishmongers and grocers competed for trade, displaying their produce with pride. Crustaceans, so fresh they crawled, super-sized fruit and vegetables and the aroma of freshly baked bread provided a feast for the senses – I started to feel hungry again. However, I wasn't in search of food, I was on the lookout for an English newspaper, but in this part of Granada they were hard to find. I did spot an *International Herald Tribune*, but the edition was two days old and I suspected that the stateside editorial wouldn't encompass much news from home. In lots of ways it was refreshing not to be able to keep up with domestic news – it made being abroad feel far more real. Anyway, I hadn't come to Spain to keep one foot in the UK, I wanted to integrate and assimilate, and I still wanted that life-changing experience.

Having made the decision that no news was good news, I gave up my quest for a 'Holy Fail' and headed back to the flat. I picked up my Hemingway and returned to the balcony, armed with a cup of tea. Well, I couldn't give up all links to home, some things are sacred. While the Hemingway delivered, the tea was a less than delicious brew – UHT milk doesn't do tea any great favours. Feeling disappointed, I spent some time contemplating the mystery of why a country that appreciates fresh food doesn't drink fresh milk, and then I spent some more time contemplating Robert Jordan's fate – I think I now know for whom the bell tolled.

One of the real joys of youth is having time to waste. Introspective, self-indulgent and generally pointless meditation continued, until Ariana returned and the next stage of the day began. We decided to head out, grab some lunch and explore the city streets of Granada. The Spanish live on the streets – home is for sleeping and occasionally eating, but the streets are for everything else. Drinking and eating out in Spain was relatively cheap, sometimes cheaper than drinking and eating at home. We caught a bus and headed into the city centre. We grabbed some *bocadillos* and then grabbed some chairs outside a bar in the Plaza Nueva. Drinks were more expensive than in the outskirts of the city, but wine or a small draft beer still only cost the equivalent of about 12p. I wasn't entirely sure that drinking so soon after suffering was a good idea, but the location and the general ambience legislated against abstinence. Built over the River Darro, the plaza used to be used for tournaments, bullfights and executions, now it was used to preen and parade – a place to see and be seen in. The setting was fantastic, we were surrounded by elegant buildings: the Royal Chancellery and the Iglesia de Santa Ana, to name but two. We sat and watched the world go by as we talked and laughed, and we made one drink last for the best part of an afternoon.

Just a small point of interest, but in Spain, just as in the UK, the afternoon officially starts at noon. Most Spaniards, however, take the afternoon to mean after lunch, and in Spain, lunch (*comida*) is usually eaten at about 2 p.m. If greeting someone you should use '*buenos dias*' before midday or before the midday meal, and '*buenas tardes*' in the afternoon. The afternoon becomes the night when the sun sets and from then on, it's '*buenas noches*'. In terms of meals and eating, the Spanish operate on a seventeen-hour day. Breakfast (*desayuno*) is usually taken at 7 a.m., with a snack at about 10:30, to tide you over until lunch. After lunch another light meal or snack may be eaten at about 6:30, and dinner (*cena*) may be taken any time from about 10 p.m. onwards. What about the children? I hear you say. Well, children usually eat with the adults and it's not uncommon to see babies, toddlers and teenagers settling down with their parents for a meal at 11 p.m. On special occasions, such as Christmas or New Year's Eve, families tend to eat at midnight. If you're going to Spain, you may have to reprogramme your constitution.

Effortlessly adapting to cafe culture, we found it difficult to drag ourselves away from the Plaza Nueva, but we thought that we should dedicate at least some of the afternoon to exploring more than just the bars of Granada. Street map in hand, we set off to explore the crumbling beauty of the Albaicin. We wandered through ancient narrow streets and climbed ever higher until we arrived at the Mirador San Nicolas – a small raised square in front of San Nicolas Church. The square offered fantastic panoramic views of the city centre, the distant Sierra Nevada mountains and the Alhambra. The area was empty, so we enjoyed the tranquillity of solitude and took our time to take everything in. The Alhambra looked stunning, equally as spectacular by day as it had been by night. I may not have been able to fully appreciate the fine architectural details from afar, but the grand scale and majesty of the building was revealed in all its glory. I stood and stared and I wished I'd brought my camera.

Committing the view to memory rather than film, I took one long last look across to the Alhambra, and then we headed back the way we had come. Slaves to appetite – hunger and a chill in the air precipitated our departure. Resisting the temptation to eat out, we decided to head back to the flat – evening meals were usually enjoyed at home. I can't remember whether we ate fried potatoes and meat or a Spanish risotto, but it was always one of the two, and both were always carefully prepared on our small, *butano*-powered gas hob. Satisfied and satiated, wined and dined, we gazed out from the balcony and watched the sunset.

Dusk was our cue to head into the streets once again. Returning to my breakfast bar, I was greeted by name, well, nationality – '*Hola* England' – it was nice to be remembered. My breakfast bar and the other local bars offered cheap wine and occasionally some free snacks – nothing too exciting, generally a few olives or some sunflower seeds. We didn't always continue on from the local bars, but tonight they were the starting point for the evening to come.

Our night continued in the city centre. We met up with some of Ariana's Spanish friends, fellow students from the University of Granada. Conversations raged at high volume and I tried to follow the gist of things. After a few drinks the general consensus was that we should find a club. Having decided to make another evening of it, we headed towards the gypsy caves of Sacromonte. Arriving at two in the morning, we danced until dawn. We wouldn't have dreamed of going to a club before two in the morning and we seldom left before five.

Tired, but thankfully feeling far healthier than the night before, I paid the taxi driver and we walked towards our flat. Rooftops were bathed in the red, orange, yellow and the brilliant white light of an Andalusian sunrise – the colours were incredible. I gave a friendly nod to the '*butano* man' and wished a warm '*buenos dias*' to some street cleaners, before heading inside, going to bed and making myself a false promise to come home a bit earlier next time.

RONDA

THIS IS NOW

Ronda must be one of the most spectacularly located towns anywhere in the world. Perched on a rocky isolated outcrop, the town straddles a precipitous limestone gorge that drops sheer for 130 metres. The river gorge is called El Tajo, though the river is El Guadalvin. Spanning the gap created by the gorge is the Puente Nuevo or 'New Bridge'. Started in 1751, the bridge took forty-two years to complete and its construction cost fifty-two lives. It is one of the most photographed spots in the whole of Spain, and it's not difficult to see why. A low arch supports three much higher arches, much like a multi-tiered Roman aqueduct. The solid blocks of stone used to build the bridge blend into the vertiginous sides of the gorge. The bridge rises majestically, soaring into the air and proving that sometimes, man-made structures can be as impressive as nature.

The Puente Nuevo dominates Ronda, and it dominated our visit. After several days of glorious inactivity, we forced ourselves to temporarily abandon Casa Mesto, and braved the mountain roads which lead to the mountainous eyrie. We entered the town from the south side, via La Ciudad, Ronda's oldest quarter. The area still retains its Moorish layout and includes many original houses. We walked through a maze of ancient streets, passing fabulous dwellings, palaces and churches as we headed towards the Puente Nuevo. We walked across the bridge and admired the extensive views over the surrounding countryside. From the bridge, it was easy to understand why Ronda was one of the last Moorish strongholds in Spain to fall to the Christian forces, only succumbing in 1485, just seven years before the fall of Granada.

Pedestrians can walk along both sides of the bridge; we darted from one side to the other, crossing a cobbled street whilst being careful to avoid the near constant stream of traffic. Both sides offered fantastic views and we were pleased to be able to optimise our viewing pleasure. The bridge has seating positions built into it, but the seats weren't being used for sitting. We joined fellow tourists in using the seats as handy steps from which to lean over the sides of the bridge and take photos. Will, Tom and Tania snapped away, but I didn't take many pictures and I didn't look for too long.

The Puente Nuevo has become infamous as a result of Hemingway's *For Whom the Bell Tolls*. In his book, Hemingway describes the execution of Nationalist supporters and sympathisers early in the Spanish Civil War. The Republicans kill Nationalists by throwing them from cliffs in an Andalusian village. Hemingway allegedly based the account on killings that took place in Ronda at the cliffs of Tajo, but there is little evidence to support the claim.

Atrocities undeniably took place on both sides, but it seems more likely that at Ronda, the Nationalists who were executed were shot behind the cemetery gates. Whilst probably fiction rather than fact, I found it impossible not to think about Hemingway's chilling chapter and the horrific fate that awaited the condemned as I looked over the edge and into the abyss.

Hemingway experienced the Spanish Civil War at first hand, he was an ardent supporter of the Republican cause. Arriving a year after the outbreak of hostilities, he covered the conflict for the American press. Reporting on the war and travelling through the country at such a momentous time in history provided the inspiration for him to write *For Whom the Bell Tolls*. The book tells the story of Robert Jordan, an American who enlists on the Republican side in the Spanish Civil War, and travels behind enemy lines to work with Spanish guerrilla fighters. The book is magnificent, greater even than the sum of its parts. On one level it's a simple adventure story, but it's also about love, life, politics, brutality and the tragedy of war – it's one of my favourite novels. The Spanish Civil War didn't mark Hemingway's first visit to Spain. Hemingway had spent time in Pamplona in the 1920s, and he became obsessed with bullfighting and matadors. In *Death in the Afternoon*, published in 1932, Hemingway looked at the history of modern bullfighting and contemplated the nature of courage and fear. Hemingway's last trip to Spain was in 1959, during this visit he chronicled what was known as a *mano a mano* (hand to hand), a series of bullfights which pitted matadors against each other. His observations were published posthumously as *The Dangerous Summer*.

Whilst I love Hemingway's writing, I don't share his love of bullfighting. I can't abide any activity where suffering is offered up as entertainment or art. I don't understand how anyone can take pleasure from another living creature's torment. Bear baiting, fox hunting, cockfighting or bullfighting, they are all the same to me. It was with a sense of trepidation, therefore, that I headed off towards the oldest and the most revered bullring in Spain.

The Plaza de Toros looks like a gladiatorial arena, and in a way, I suppose that's just what it is, hosting similarly one-sided contests. As well as being the oldest, the bullring is one of the largest in Spain. Opened in 1785, the sand-and-clay-filled arena has a diameter of 66 metres and is surrounded by a passage formed by two rings of stone. Spectators occupy two layers of seating, each with five raised rows, fronted by 136 columns which support sixty-eight glorious arches. The arena is only used once a year for fighting, but it's an important matador training school.

With a sense of self-reproach, we paid the entrance fee, walked through an elaborate Baroque doorway and then toured the building. I hate to say so, but the place was impressive and was definitely worth a visit. I may hate bullfighting and I have a healthy disrespect for tradition, but I appreciate good architecture and I love history. Feeling guilty and hypocritical, and impressed and horrified at the same time, I fought Tom in the main arena before exploring the bull pens and a quite fascinating museum. Apparently, Ronda is the spiritual home of the modern *corrida* or bullfight, and the founder of the modern style was Francisco Romero. Before Francisco, bullfighting was an activity normally carried out from the back of a horse in what was known as the 'Jerez style'. Romero fought on foot and introduced the style that many are familiar with today.

Continuing on foot, we decided to head back towards the Puente Nuevo. Our route took us along the Paseo Hemingway, a spectacular walkway which offers fantastic views of the Puente Nuevo and the surrounding area. The views from the Mirador de Aldehuela were particularly impressive. The viewpoint occupies a small ledge which appears to float unsupported in the air as it juts out from the city walls. The viewpoint is named in honour of the architect Jose Martin de Aldehuela, who designed both the Puente Nuevo and the Plaza de Toros. Stopping frequently to admire the views and to take on water, we wandered past an elegant Parador, which was formally the town hall, before we emerged onto the Plaza de Espana; a lively and impressive square, full of hotels, restaurants and tourist shops, selling ponchos and flamenco dresses amongst many other things. Resisting the temptation to buy, we made our way downhill, past the Iglesias de Nuestro Padre Jesus and then onto the 'Old Bridge' or 'Roman Bridge' or 'Arab Bridge' – Ronda has had a long and interesting history.

Ronda is surrounded by prehistoric remains, but the area was first settled by the Celts in the early 6th century BC. The Celts (Iberians) chose the site because they thought it was impregnable – it was, until the Romans arrived. After capturing the unassailable stronghold, the Romans developed the site into a fortified outpost. Mentioned by Pliny and Ptolemy, they named the new town Arunda, which rather aptly means surrounded by mountains. Arunda flourished under Roman rule; it grew in importance and was granted city status by Julius Caesar. The Roman hold on the city lasted until the disintegration of the Roman Empire, at which stage Arunda was lost to the Vandals, who lived up to their name by completely destroying the place. The Vandals' reign in Andalusia was short-lived; they were replaced by the Visigoths, who re-established the present site of Ronda, until in 713 the area was taken and the old town was fortified by the Moors. The Moorish conquest brought only temporary stability, it didn't bring peace – these were turbulent times. The Moors divided southern Andalusia into five districts, and Ronda was fought over by different Arab factions until its reconquest by the Marquis of Cadiz. Subsequently, most of the city's old buildings were renewed or adapted to Christian roles.

Turning back the clock, we enjoyed yet more spectacular views of the gorge, before visiting the Arab Baths (Baños Arabes). Built at the end of the 13th century, the Arabic baths are said to be the best preserved in Spain. The baths comprise three rooms and the largest central room is divided into three parts by horseshoe-shaped arches and octagonal brick columns. The baths were based on the Roman model of thermal buildings, with cold, warm and hot bathrooms. Water from El Guadalvin, was delivered via an aqueduct; the water was then heated in large cauldrons which still impress today. Most impressive of all, however, was the barrel-vaulted ceiling, complete with its star-shaped vents which allowed shafts of light to pass through and illuminate the cavernous interior.

We spent more than a few moments exploring the building and we even found time to watch a film about the history and functioning of the baths. Designed to educate rather than entertain, we soaked up facts whilst enjoying the cool of the shaded interior.

The cool interior was in sharp contrast to the baking exterior – the day had warmed up significantly. Before we were thirsty, now we were parched. We struggled as we climbed back uphill and we stopped to rest outside El Palacio del Rey Moro. Legend would have us believe that this was the house of the Moorish King Almonated, who is said to have drunk wine from the jewel-encrusted skulls of his victims. The present building was built in the 18th century, so to a certain extent the house is a bit of a sham. The gardens of the house do, however, give access to the Water Mine, a staircase of Islamic origin.

It was in the 14th century that Ronda first found itself in the firing line between the Moors of Granada and the Christians of Seville. Highly sought and fought over, Ronda was frequently besieged, and the first target of every besieging army was the water supply. Using Christian captives as slave labour, Ronda's Moorish king ordered the cutting of over 300 steps into the stone walls of the gorge to enable water from El Guadalvin to be carried up to the town. Though intended as a secret, it wasn't a particularly well kept one. It is thought that it was here that the Christian troops forced entry to the city.

Dehydrated and only partially recovered, but probably feeling better than Almonated's Christian slaves, we continued the steep climb back towards El Puente Nuevo and the Plaza de Espania – it was time for lunch.

Thirst and hunger took us to the Calle Nueva – a pedestrianised street full of restaurants and cafes. Elegant three-storey buildings with wrought-iron balconies framed a bustling and clamorous scene; tables, chairs and customers completed the canvas. Restaurants tried to out-compete each other with special offers, enticing *menús del dia*, colourful tablecloths and purple prose. We were accosted rather than greeted by waiters, waitresses and proprietors as we walked from one end of the street to the other.

One particularly friendly and helpful waitress said that she could guarantee that we would not leave her house unsatisfied. Well, it was enough for me. We dined alfresco at the Restaurante Granada, on a mixture of *migas rondenas*, *pulpo a la gallagas*, *paella*, *calamares fritos* and *solomillo de cerdo*, followed by *natillas* and *helado*, all washed down by wine and water – not the first time I was reminded of why I love the *menú del dia*. Three courses, plus a drink for 11 euros – just perfect. Feeling full and satiated, we headed back to La Ciudad, and then headed for home, but I knew I would miss Ronda.

Ronda is undoubtedly one of the most beautiful places that I have ever visited, passionate and picturesque. Hemingway famously stated in *Death in the Afternoon* that: 'Ronda is the place where to go, if you are planning to travel to Spain for a honeymoon or for being with a girlfriend. The whole city and its surroundings are a romantic set ... Nice promenades, good wine, excellent food, nothing to do ...'

I can't agree with Hemingway on matters of sport, but on the subject of Ronda, I couldn't agree more.

WAR

That Was Then

'*Hijo de puta!*' Ariana cried out suddenly as she broke step and stormed into a small bar on the outskirts of Granada. 5ft2 of very angry Basque charged towards a very large barman. Collision was inevitable, but I knew who my money was on and that person didn't serve drinks. What I didn't know was the reason for the exclamation or the angry confrontation. I took a back seat and watched with interest as the battle commenced. Ariana shouted angrily and pointed towards a carved bust in the window of the bar. I caught one word, 'Franco'. Other words were lost to invective and translation. The barman, to his credit, remained calm in front of the raging storm. He pointed at the bust and said '*No es Franco es Lorca*' – I'd backed the wrong person.

Federico Garcia Lorca and Francisco Franco were about as different as two people could be. While Lorca did have some right-wing friends, he was a left-wing, modern-minded, Republican, homosexual, poet and playwright. Francisco Franco was a right-wing, Catholic, Nationalist, homicidal dictator and tyrant. They looked pretty different as well. Lorca was a clean-shaven, dark-haired, handsome, full-faced man, while Franco was a moustachioed, balding, shrivelled man, with the sort of face that only a mother could love. The two men, strikingly dissimilar in just about every way, encapsulated many of the opposing views and characteristics that tore Spain apart in the Spanish Civil War.

To be fair to Ariana, the bust in the bar didn't look like Lorca, but then again it didn't look like Franco either. In many ways it was an easy mistake to make, but in a modernising democratic and left-wing Spain, it was a contentious mistake. The depiction of Franco, or for that matter Lorca, could not just divide opinion, it could polarise it. The Left were on the ascendency and the country had a euphoric and optimistic feel about it, but the Right still had a considerable amount of support. Franco may not have had a son and heir, but his movement and politics had been inherited by many. Spain now has a policy of forgiving and forgetting, but scratch the surface and people remember and blame – the country still bleeds. In 1984, Spain could only really be understood in the context of its tumultuous past.

Spain in the early 20th century was not a united country. Opposites attract, but they generally repel; lines were drawn. Left against right, republicanism against monarchism, secularism against Catholicism, regionalism against nationalism, personal freedom against centralised control, communism against fascism, socialism against conservatism, rural against urban, the landless proletariat against the landowners, poor against rich and modernism against traditionalism. Politics and allegiances were all important. Resentment and antagonism led to anger and fear, groups began to join forces. Affiliations led to broad coalitions, sides were taken, daggers were drawn. If you weren't with one side, you were with the other.

The lack of unity between the many factions and forces in Spain had its origins in a number of different social and economic issues. Spain had suffered a long period of decline since the days of Empire. Most of Spain's possessions in Latin America had become independent in the early 19th century, and those that remained were lost to the US, in the Spanish-American War of 1898. Only a small stretch of North Africa, Spanish Morocco, was left of the empire that had once ruled half the world and brought untold wealth into the Spanish coffers. Economic depression led to a degree of spiritual despondency, as the Spanish lost confidence in their own nation and their national identity. Military defeats added to the nations woes, but the military felt that they were unjustifiably held responsible for the country's failings. Spain lagged behind the rest of Europe industrially and socially. Huge wealth gaps existed and a sense of faded glory prevailed as ideological divisions widened. The Church opposed social reform and landowners failed to embrace or competitively exploit industrialisation. The Spanish wanted a new future, but they weren't sure which type of future they wanted. Unrest began to spread and Spain's internal contradictions fuelled the flames.

Discontent, strikes, unrest, poverty, economic recession and a fear of democracy inspired General Primo de Rivera to launch a coup d'état in 1923. His right-wing military dictatorship was supported by the king, but it was mindful of the need to reform. Primo de Rivera, however, found that reform was more difficult to instigate than he had imagined. The general ended up upsetting both Left and Right. Too reforming for some and too slow to reform for others, he initially kept a firm grip on the country, but his ultimate legacy was more disunity. Forced to resign in 1930, after he managed to lose the support of the army that he had once led, Primo de Rivera left the scene. Conservatives lost the initiative as reformers gained the ascendency and the right to free elections. Spain was beginning to change.

Municipal elections were held in April 1931. In the cities and towns, Republicans and Socialists were triumphant and they demanded the king's abdication. When the army withdrew its support, King Alphonso XIII's days were numbered. Alphonso's subsequent departure from Spain marked the beginning of the Second Spanish Republic. Alcala Zamora was declared as provisional president, and in October 1931, Manuel Azana became prime minister. The Republican government brought in a series of overdue, but controversial reforms. Church and State were separated; education would no longer be controlled by the Catholic hierarchy. The army would be overhauled. Civil marriage was instituted and divorce was allowed. Woman were given the vote. Minority languages were recognised and Catalonia was granted autonomy.

Catholic and right-wing supporters within the country were horrified by the changes and by the speed of change. The army, faced with cuts in pay and numbers, revolted in 1932. The revolt was crushed, but the resentment and anti-reformist dissatisfaction that had inspired the rising was not. The Right became more organised. The Catholic CEDA party and the Falange, a fascist party led by the son of Primo de Rivera, Jose Antonio Primo de Rivera, were both set up. At the same time, shifting allegiances within the Republic resulted in the Socialists refusing to participate in government – Zamora was forced to dissolve parliament.

The Right joined forces to fight the 1933 general election. The tactics worked and the Right triumphed. The new government reversed the process of reform and cancelled measures taken against the Church. These actions galvanised the Left. In 1934, a general strike was called in opposition to the government and an anarchist miners' revolt took place in Asturias. The miners were eventually defeated, but only after a brutal military intervention led by the army's new rising star, General Franco. Mass arrests of left-wing sympathisers followed and left-wing newspapers were closed down. At the same time, Catalonia's autonomous status was suspended. Spanish politics became even more polarised.

In 1936, an election was called. Angered by the Right, a Popular Front of Communists, Socialists and Republicans was formed to oppose the government. The Popular Front believed that another victory for the Right would lead to fascism. The right-wing National Front believed that victory for the Left would lead to communism.

The Popular Front narrowly won the election, succeeding primarily in urban areas. The new government proceeded to reintroduce earlier reforms. See-saw politics had dominated the scene, but they were a recipe for disaster. Both sides now feared the worst, disorder and political violence spread throughout the country. Peasants seized land and there were many strikes. The Falange started to grow dramatically as disillusioned supporters of the more moderate CEDA joined its ranks. Its members used political violence and based their actions on Nazi tactics – attack and counterattack became common. The Church vehemently opposed the government. The army, with the support of the Church hierarchy, began plotting another coup d'état. Spain was ready to explode, all that was required was a spark.

On 13 July 1936, the right-wing monarchist politician Calvo Sotelo was assassinated by Republicans in revenge for the murder of one or their men by a Falangist. The fuse had already been lit, but the chaos that followed the murders provided the army with an excuse to put their pre-planned plot into action. Army units, dancing to the tune of General Emilio Mola, rose simultaneously across Spain.

Mola assumed that victory would be swift, but he was mistaken – he had overestimated the power of his own rhetoric and underestimated the power of the people. Although the bulk of the army rebelled, many units stayed loyal to the elected government and a people's army rose to support the Republic, arming itself and fighting back under anarchist, socialist and communist leadership.

The rebels took swift control of the conservative and Catholic areas of Old Castile and Leon, as well as the cities of Granada, Cordoba and crucially Seville, which would provide a landing point for Franco, who had flown to Morocco to take charge of the African troops. Industrial cities, however, which housed large numbers of politically active left-wing workers, rallied against the Right. In areas where the workers were armed by the Republic, successful defence was possible. In Madrid, street fighting was fierce and communist leader Dolares Ibarruri, La Pasionaria, urged resistance with her rallying cry of '*No Pasaran*' – 'They will not pass'. After much bloodshed, Madrid was held for the government, along with Barcelona and Valencia. In terms of territory, the Republic retained control of Asturias, Santander, the Basque Country, much of the east coast and the Central region around Madrid, as well as Malaga, Jaen and Almería in Andalusia.

After the initial terror of the uprising, the Nationalists and Republicans began to organise their respective areas of control, both sides began to repress opposition or suspected opposition – a new reign of terror began. Republican violence occurred mainly in the early stages of the war, in a random and fairly disorganised way before the rule of law was restored. Nationalist violence was part of a conscious, well-planned and methodical policy. The Right were determined to eliminate all opposition, current or potential. Class and political repression took place, 'ideological cleansing' to create a new Spain, was the new order of the day.

As dawn broke over a broken Spain, the world looked on with interest. The plight of Republican Spain had captured the imagination of all, the Spanish Civil War had become much more than a national conflict. The Civil War, based on intransigent domestic contradictions, was part of a larger international conflict of ideologies, between left and right, tyranny and democracy, fascism and communism – Spain was a microcosm for world events.

As the world looked on, the Republicans and Nationalists looked to the world for support. Both sides knew that they were too weak to win an outright victory without help, but where would that help come from?

The UK government was more pro-Nationalist than not, but advised a policy of non-intervention. A non-intervention pact was agreed by Britain, and twenty-four other nations, including France, Germany, the Soviet Union and Italy in August 1936. The British wanted to protect their business interests and they didn't want to provoke either Germany or Italy, but public opinion supported the Republic. France, a fellow left-wing republic, was naturally sympathetic to Spain, and lent support at the beginning of the conflict, but the French didn't want to upset the British, because they were concerned about the possibility of future German aggression. Germany didn't want to fully provoke Britain, because Germany wasn't fully militarised yet, but Hitler was a natural ally of the Nationalists and he didn't want the Republic to succeed, because the Republic would be a natural ally of France. Hitler already thought that confrontation with France was inevitable. Hitler had also been advised that Spain would be a good testing ground for his troops, tactics and weapons, so he agreed to non-intervention, whilst supplying the Nationalists with military aid. The Soviet Union, perhaps surprisingly, didn't want an out-and-out communist revolution in Spain, Stalin knew that this would make the British and the French feel threatened, and he realised that he would need British and French support in the event of war with Germany. Stalin didn't, however, want a fascist victory in Spain, because this would affect the balance of power in Europe.

Stalin wanted the Republic to succeed, but realised that his best outcome was a protracted war which would tie everyone down and allow the Soviet Union to strengthen its position. Stalin signed up to non-intervention, but supplied the Republic with planes and tanks when he realised that Germany and Italy were supplying the Nationalists and that a fascist victory was imminent in the autumn of 1936. Mussolini, in Italy, saw himself as the founding father of fascism and consequently wanted to support and did support the Nationalists; he also wanted to prove himself to Hitler, despite his own inflated sense of self-importance. Mexico, a fellow left-wing republic, supported the elected Spanish government. The plight of the Republic also attracted some 40,000 individual volunteers from over fifty different nations; usually socialists, communists or anarchists, sometimes simply idealists, they fought for the Republican side as members of the international brigades or local militias. Included amongst their number were George Orwell and Laurie Lee.

The Spanish Civil War had gone way beyond the confines of a national conflict. Non-intervention was official policy, but interference was everywhere, the die had been cast.

With the outcome of the Civil War hanging in the balance, the Nationalists were more than a little anxious to get their Africa troops into the fray. Isolated on the wrong side of the Mediterranean, with the Republic in control of the navy, Franco faced a bit of a problem. The end of July, however, heralded a very decisive piece of non-interventional interference: Hitler provided transport planes to transfer Franco and his army from Morocco to Seville. This was the first military airlift of its kind to take place anywhere in the world, and it left the Republic at a distinct disadvantage. By the beginning of August, the Nationalists had enough troops at their disposal to be able to leave Seville, take Badajoz, and march towards Madrid. By contrast, the Republic was on the defensive as they attempted to turn their ragtag loose association of regular troops, loyal police offices and militia volunteers into an effective fighting force.

The Nationalist push was on, but Franco wasn't in any hurry. Much to the alarm of some of his supporters, Franco, cautious by nature, favoured a slow campaign. Franco didn't just want to defeat the opposition, he wanted to eradicate it. While the main body of his troops marched towards Madrid, his occupying troops began their mission of identification and elimination. On 19 August, Lorca was executed in Granada. Recently unearthed documents confirm that Lorca was executed for his beliefs; arresting officers described him as a socialist, a homosexual and a Freemason. Lorca's execution was sadly just one amongst many, but his death was publicised around the world as the fascist murder of a socialist poet. His violent end galvanised support and focused the eyes of the world even more closely on Spain. The murder of Lorca, undoubtable helped recruitment for the International Brigades, and reinforced resistance, as Republicans realised the fate that awaited them if captured by the Nationalists.

While Franco controlled the Nationalist army in the south, Mola had control in the north. By September, the Nationalists in the north had captured Irun, effectively isolating the rest of the Basque Country from other Republican-controlled areas and from France. Isolation was absolute, the Basque coastline was blockaded by non-intervention countries, who in theory were there to ensure fair play. Unable to resupply by land or sea, the Basques were now completely alone.

Increasingly unchallenged, the overall leadership of the Nationalists was gradually assumed by Franco, as his rivals either lost authority or lost their lives. By the end of September, Franco had declared himself Generalissimo, and he was declared Head of State shortly afterwards. The Republican government was headed by the socialist leader Francisco Largo Caballero. He would be followed in May 1937 by Juan Negrín, also a socialist. The president of the Spanish Republic until nearly the end of the war was Azana.

Dictating policy, Franco delayed attacking Madrid, which was at its weakest, and turned his attention to Toledo instead. Toledo fell, but the delay was crucial. Time allowed Madrid to strengthen its defences, which were also bolstered by the arrival of Soviet supplies and the first of the International Brigades. By the time the Nationalists turned their attention back to Madrid, the city was stronger and the people were even more resolute and resolved. In November, dogged Republican resistance, combined with Soviet planes and tanks, forced the Nationalists to abandon their attempt to take the city. The arrival of Soviet supplies and influence may, however, have had at least one negative consequence, which epitomised Republican infighting. Buenaventura Durruti, a charismatic, anarcho-syndicalist leader, was killed during the battle for Madrid, possibly by communist forces. The anarchist and communists were unlikely bedfellows, internal power struggles hampered any prospect of a fully unified defence.

The beginning of 1937 saw yet more attempts by the Nationalists to capture Madrid, but they had missed their chance. The new year brought death, destruction and stalemate. The Nationalists probed for weaknesses and the Republicans defended with determination. Both sides eventually accepted the inevitable: they dug trenches and settled in for a long siege. The siege of Madrid would last for another two years.

Frustrated outside Madrid, the Nationalists turned their focus back to Andalusia, and launched an offensive on Malaga. Marching from Seville and Granada, Malaga presented a very different proposition to Madrid. The city was dominated by Anarchists, who hadn't organised any effective defence. There weren't any trenches or roadblocks or anti-aircraft weapons, and there wasn't any real Soviet support. Horrified by the prospect of an invading well-armed force of Moors, Italians and right-wing militia, accompanied by tanks and planes, about 100,000 people fled the city. The exodus, slowed down by the wounded and sheer numbers, was mercilessly attacked from both the air and the sea. Strafed by planes and shelled by ships, thousands of people died; combatants and non-combatants, men and women, old and young – this was total war. Those trying to escape Malaga fared little better than those that remained. Mass executions of suspected socialists took place, accompanied by indiscriminate rape – the Italians were horrified by the scale of the violence.

In March, the Italians tried to encircle Madrid, but they were defeated at the Battle of Guadalajara. After what turned out to be the only publicised Republican victory of the war, Franco turned his attention back to the Basque Country. The Basques lacked support, but not tenacity. Recently granted autonomy, the Basques of Álava, Guipúzcoa and Biscay were fighting not just for the Republic, but for their independence. The Basques prepared their defences, but they had little air cover and they couldn't have foreseen the ferocity of the approaching storm. Franco was about to unleash the German Condor Legion, and the world was about to discover the horror and terror of Blitzkrieg. On 26 April, the town of Guernica, the spiritual capital of the Basque people, was subjected to three hours of near continuous carpet bombing. Non-military targets were attacked, it was market day, it was carnage. After the first wave of bombers had passed, civilians returned to search for friends and family, only to find themselves the target of a second and then a third wave of attack. This was terror bombing, a new form of warfare which deliberately targeted civilians to break morale and the will to resist. The number of casualties is disputed, but at least 300 people are thought to have died in the rubble and flames of the ruined town. Many more people literally scraped their fingers to the bone as they searched for loved ones amongst the debris of destruction. Guernica changed public opinion, as once again Spain found itself in the spotlight. World reaction turned many former pro-Nationalists against Franco and his allies. Guernica became a global symbol of civilian suffering and inspired Picasso to create and display his most famous work. Picasso used black and white paint, newspaper cuttings and stark imagery to invoke the horror of the attack. His painting, simply called *Guernica*, was displayed in Paris at the World Fair, between March and November – it forced viewers to face up to the reality of modern warfare. Unfortunately, whilst public opinion shifted, the world's politicians didn't face up to the reality of the situation. Non-intervention was still the order of the day and Franco's tactics, although not directly endorsed, were tacitly tolerated.

'If you tolerate this, then your children will be next' – the Republic used this slogan, below the sightless eyes and the lifeless body of a young girl, to publicise the reality of non-intervention and to show the future which awaited other democracies if fascism was allowed to triumph in Spain – it's a shame that the world didn't listen – world peace, it transpired, wasn't their business.

During the months of May and June, the Basques were slowly forced back towards Bilbao. Now fully aware of the ferocity of the of the ongoing storm, they tried to evacuate their children. In total 20,000 would leave Spain for safe havens. At first, Britain refused the appeal to offer temporary asylum to the Basque children, citing non-intervention, but after the Duchess of Atholl took up their cause and public opinion backed her campaign, 4,000 were eventually allowed to enter the UK. The British government, however, refused to finance the operation; the excuse, once again, was the non-intervention agreement. It's hard to imagine the heartbreak felt by the children or their families as they left Spain, not knowing when or if they would return, or what would face them in the UK. 'Los ninos' arrived on 23 May, on the steamship SS *Habana*. Disembarking in Southampton, the children were housed at a temporary camp in Eastleigh, before being dispersed to all four corners of the country and various destinations in between. Most of the children were repatriated after the war, but 250 remained, their parents either missing, dead or imprisoned. Among the 250 children who stayed in the UK, hoping to build a new life, were

Ariana's mother, father and her aunt – it's little wonder that the mere thought of Franco could stir such strong emotions.

The Nationalists continued their advance. The Basque army, fighting a defensive action, hoped to position themselves inside the 'Iron Ring' – a vast fortification of bunkers, tunnels and trenches arranged in several rings around Bilbao. Unfortunately, the layout of the Ring was betrayed to the Nationalist army by the very person who had designed it. Consequently, the Condor Legion was able to obliterate its defensive capabilities. The Nationalists broke through and occupied the high ground above Bilbao, the Basques retreated towards Santander.

In an attempt to alleviate the pressure exerted by the Nationalists on the Basques and on Madrid, the Republic planned the Brunete offence to the west of Madrid. Initially successful, the Republicans were eventually forced to give up most of the ground they gained and in the process, they lost irreplaceable lives and invaluable equipment. Whilst some Nationalist troops had been transferred from the north to fight at Brunete, relief for the north was only temporary. By the beginning of August, Basque resistance was in its death throes; the inevitable had merely been delayed.

By the end of August, Santander was under Nationalist control. Hitler's 'non-intervention' earned Germany the right to two-thirds of all mine and steel production from the Basque Country. Pushing inexorably onwards, Asturias was the next region to fall to Franco. After a heroic defence, Nationalists entered the city of Gijon, killing and raping with impunity. The war in the north was effectively over. The Republic, which had moved its government from Madrid to Valencia, moved again to Barcelona; the war was heading east and the Republic was heading for disaster.

In yet another attempt to distract Franco from Madrid, the Republicans launched an offensive aimed at capturing the Aragonese provincial capital of Teruel. Fighting took place in ice and snow, blizzards caused frostbite and hampered troop movements on both sides as the worst winter in twenty years struck home. The Republic didn't hold back, they committed 100,000 men and by Christmas they had successfully entered the city, but it wasn't to be a 'Happy New Year'. Franco stubbornly refused to admit defeat and wouldn't countenance the loss of any territory. Pouring men and equipment into a counterattack, while still holding troops, tanks and planes in reserve, the Nationalists encircled and then recaptured the city.

Teruel was a disaster for the Republic. An initial morale-boosting victory was quickly countered by retreat and defeat. While it's thought that the Nationalists' casualties were about 56,000, the Republic lost nearly 85,000 men and most of their remaining aircraft. The Battle for Teruel exhausted the resources of the Republican army and increased the likelihood of a successful Nationalist breakthrough to the Mediterranean – it was the beginning of the end.

The likelihood of a successful breakthrough to the Mediterranean soon became a reality. In March 1938, the Nationalists launched the Aragon offensive and they quickly captured large amounts of territory. Franco was able to call upon more reserves, while what was left of the Republican army was in disarray. The Nationalists reached the Mediterranean coast in April, and effectively split the Republic in two. The Republic attempted to negotiate for peace, but Franco demanded nothing less than unconditional surrender – the war rumbled on.

Upon reaching the coast, Franco turned his attention towards Valencia. Initially successful, the Nationalist advance was slowed by staunch resistance and then postponed because the Republican army, to the surprise of all, launched the Ebro offensive.

Achieving almost total surprise, Republican troops crossed the Ebro River in a massive operation to re-establish a link between the two separate Republican zones and to relieve pressure on Valencia. Surprise was possible, because the reopening of the French/Spanish border, and an extended call-up, enabled the Republic to create and supply a new army far more quickly than anyone thought possible. For Negrin, who planned the battle, the offensive was also an attempt to prolong the war. Tensions in Europe were high and Negrin hoped that a full scale European war would break out before Franco achieved total victory in Spain. Negrin's belief that the allies would directly or indirectly come to his aid whilst fighting the forces of fascism was, however, sadly quashed by the Munich agreement. Czechoslovakia's defensive frontier, the Sudetenland, was surrendered in exchange for Chamberlain's 'Peace for our time'. Unfortunately, time was running out.

The Battle of the Ebro became a war of attrition and for the Republic, it was the last throw of the dice. The battle, which began in July and ended in November, was the longest and largest of the war. The element of surprise led to early success, but Franco was quick to respond, committing heavy reinforcements to counter the Republican threat. Further Republican advances soon became impossible and by crossing the Ebro, the Republic hampered its ability to be able to resupply its own front-line troops. Forced to hold on to captured ground at any cost, the Republican army was eventually overcome by superior weaponry and weight of numbers. Forced to retreat, back across the Ebro, the Republic lost most of what little was left of its equipment. Future defence was fully compromised, the gamble had failed.

Realising that the end was nigh, Franco followed up his victory at the Ebro River with a massive assault on Catalonia. Overwhelmed and under-armed, Republican resistance collapsed and the Republican government fled the country. The Nationalists swept all before them and Barcelona fell on 26 January. Hundreds of thousands of Republican soldiers, men, women, children and elderly non-combatants marched towards the French frontier, enduring bitterly cold conditions. Though offered some protection by units of the Republican army, the refugees were bombed and strafed by the Nationalist Air Force and the Condor Legion. The Nationalists reached the frontier on 9 February. By the end of February, Britain and France had both officially recognised Franco's government – Madrid and the south-east were all that remained of the once proud Republic.

By March, resolve and revolutionary spirit had finally broken and the Republican army rose against its own prime minister, Juan Negrin. The army attempted to negotiate a peace deal with the Nationalists. The communists rose in retaliation against the army and started a civil war within the civil war. The communists were defeated, but Franco refused the overtures of peace offered by the Republican army. Weakened by years of fighting and infighting, Madrid finally fell on 28 March, and by 31 March, the Nationalists controlled the whole of Spain. The dream was over – Franco declared victory on 1 April 1939.

The dream may have been over and the war had officially ended, but for many people, pain, suffering and struggle would linger on. Franco certainly didn't have a policy of forgiving and forgetting, his enemies faced harsh reprisals. Repression, executions, brutality, imprisonment, forced labour and forced ideology would provide the framework for Franco's 'new' Spain. Few former Republicans or their families would be left untouched. Ariana's parents and her aunt were stranded in the UK, her uncle only managed to escape Franco's retribution by rowing around the coast and into France, and her grandfather, arrested for producing anti-Nationalist pamphlets, would die in prison.

The Nationalists had won, and Franco and Francoism were the result. A vision of a new tomorrow had been replaced with the actuality of an archaic past. For Ariana, and for many like her, it's a past that's impossible to forget.

THIS IS NOW

Relaxing at Casa Mesto, I took advantage of the free Wi-Fi and logged onto the BBC news website. I was surprised to see the following headline:

Spanish dictator Franco names to go from Madrid streets.

Back in 1984, I had presumed that Franco's memory had already been officially erased from Spain and Spanish history. I thought that if Francoist statues, pictures or symbols still existed, they would be in private collections, residences or businesses, not public spaces. But, how wrong I was; I must have been walking around with my eyes closed. Although most statues of Franco were removed in the 1980s, it was only in 2007 that a Historical Memory Law called for the removal of all symbols relating to the 1939–75 dictatorship. However, many such symbols still exist. Apparently, in 2015, some 170 street names in Madrid alone referred to the names of dictatorship officials. Calle General Yague is a major street name in Madrid, yet Yague is commonly referred to as the 'Butcher of Badajoz' – he oversaw the massacre of approximately 4,000 Republicans in the Plaza de Toros. Calle de los Caídos de la División Azul was named in honour of Franco's Blue Division forces, which fought alongside the Nazis between 1941 and 1943. Calle Garcia Alted commemorates the general who ordered merciless air and sea attacks on civilians fleeing Malaga, and then systematically rounded up and killed thousands of others. When you think about it, it's not just bizarre, it's insulting – it would be like having a Heinrich Himmler street in Berlin. Apart from street names, some schools, health centres, and towns and villages have been named after Franco or figures connected to his regime. Symbolic engravings, memorial arches and Franco's own memorial to himself, the 'Valley of the Fallen', still exist. Ariana's confrontation aside, it has become apparent on my various trips to Spain that most Spaniards simply don't mention Franco or the Civil War, so it's strange that such historical memorabilia still exists. While many in Spain are outraged that the Historical Memory Law has not been fully acted upon, almost as many people object to the law. Presumably they don't want Franco or Francoism to be forgotten.

If you scratch the surface and delve into the past, Spain is still a divided nation.

LOST WEEKENDS
Motril and Jerez de la Frontera

That Was Then

After a few too many late nights, we decided to take a break and headed to the coast for a few more. Our destination was Motril. Excited by the prospect of exploring somewhere new, I was less than excited by the prospect of another coach trip. My sense of foreboding was justified. The journey was interminable. In 1984, the trip generally took about two hours, as coaches, cars and lorries slowly wound their way up, down and around the narrow mountain roads that separated sea and sierra. Spain was not just divided by politics, but by mountains and poor infrastructure. Two hours of sheer drops and searing heat in a cramped coach would have been bad enough, but our journey took nearly four hours. The coach broke down en route and a replacement had to be found.

Arriving in Motril somewhat later than expected, we sought out some accommodation. Ariana suggested a *hostal*. I had visions of bunk beds and dormitories, but *hostales* in Spain are different to youth hostels. *Hostales* are small, independently run hotels and they are classified from one to three stars – youth hostels aren't classified at all. We chose a clean and tidy room in a modern building. Recently decorated and complete with an en suite bathroom, it was (at the time) the best room that I had ever paid to stay in, and we didn't pay very much – surely there had to be some kind of catch?

Located on a hill, Motril is the largest town on the Costa Tropical – the Mediterranean coastline of the province of Granada. The town boasts a long history and is home to many interesting sights. Ignoring all of them, we grabbed some food and drink, and headed straight towards the Playa Granada. Disregarding antiquity and architecture, we paid attention to sea, sun, sand and each other. Youth isn't necessarily wasted on the young, but some of the more cultural aspects of travel are.

We drank, ate, talked, sunbathed, paddled and read. The sand and shingle beach may not have been one of the nicest that I have ever visited, but not much can beat lazing around on a sunny afternoon. I'm not sure that I believe in an

afterlife, but if a heavenly paradise does exist, then I hope it involves endless days of reading good books and supping cold beer whilst waves gently lap your feet and the sun warms your body – that's my kind of promised land. Even at the time, I knew that this was a good time. I remember thinking that life couldn't get much better than this. I was young, I was healthy, I was doing exactly what I wanted to do, and I was exactly where I wanted to be. Worries and responsibilities belonged to another time, a future time and a past that no longer figured – I was alive to possibilities.

Perceptive and ready to respond to all that life could offer, I carried on reading and we stayed on the beach for quite some time. I could happily have stayed for much longer, but time and tide wait for no man. Incoming waves began to threaten our position and the burning sun began to threaten our health – we headed back into town.

I remember walking along palm-tree-lined streets and passing beside beautiful old Moorish buildings, but some areas of Motril were less than enchanting. All too often, old and new were poorly integrated. Franco's use of American military base cash to support a rapidly expanding tourist industry led to many planning disasters in many areas of Spain. The Left in Spain had hung on to the possibility that the allied nations would take on Franco at the end of the Second World War, but as time passed this dream faded. It became increasing apparent that a fear of communism overrode fears of fascism. In the late 1940s and early 1950s, the United States government took steps to normalise its political and economic relationship with Spain. President Truman supported a UN resolution to lift boycotts on Franco's regime and resume full diplomatic relations; he also signed a bill that secured $62.5 million worth of aid. Nationalist, anti-communist Spain had become an increasingly important link in the overall defence system of the United States against the Soviet Union. In 1953, Franco signed the Pact of Madrid. The pact consisted of three separate, but interdependent agreements between Spain and the United States. It provided for mutual defence, for military aid to Spain, and for the construction of military bases in Spain. The Cold War was a profitable business for Franco. The deal was initially agreed upon for a period of ten years. During this time, Spain received $1.5 billion worth of aid. The agreement was subsequently renewed, and some military bases are now permanent. The deal between the 'Land of the Free' and a dictatorship further legitimised Franco's position – so much for democracy.

After assessing some of the sights of Motril, we democratically decided to return to the *hostal*. Our plan was to freshen up, head out, find something to eat and drink, and then retire for a relatively early night and a long sleep. The plan almost worked. Washed and ready to go, we explored bars and restaurants, before heading back to the *hostal* at pretty much the same time that we usually headed out in Granada. The cumulative effect of a string of late nights and excessive alcohol consumption had eroded our reserves – we headed to bed.

Fully asleep, only moments after my head hit the pillow, I was awoken by what appeared to be a seismic tremor. The whole room shook with a violence that legislated against slumber. The floor and the bed reverberated in four-four time. I had flashbacks to old geography lessons. Andalusia is situated next to a tectonic plate margin; I thought about leaping out of bed and attempting to duck, cover and hold. Bright, vibrant, multicoloured lights flashed and illuminated the room – I presumed that the emergency services were stepping into action. Things suddenly went quiet, objects stopped shaking and I thought I heard a tannoy announcing instructions or a warning. I listened intently. 'This is the sound. When you hear the air attack warning. You and your family must take cover.' A familiar bass riff kicked into action and the room started to shake again. This wasn't an earthquake or the outbreak of hostilities, but 'Two Tribes' were going to war; an aural offensive had broken out and I had discovered 'the catch' with our room. What was it with Spain and Frankie Goes to Hollywood? Holly Johnson's voice burst into our room and nearly burst my eardrums. The catch? Our *hostal* was semi-detached, and our neighbour was a nightclub.

Sleep was impossible; impossible for everyone, that is, apart from Ariana – she only woke when I asked her if she was still asleep. Moments later, after receiving an angry rebuke, sleep was impossible for both of us. 'Two Tribes' may have faded out, but a succession of other tunes faded in. Surmising that 'if you can't beat them, you might as well join them', we abandoned bed and embraced the night. Rather appropriately, we dressed to Wham's 'Wake Me Up Before You Go Go' and rather less appropriately (there wasn't a full moon and France was fair few miles away) we headed out to the strains of 'Lobo-Hombre En Paris' (Wolf Man in Paris) by La Union.

THIS IS NOW

After one of our more successful navigational approaches, we arrived on schedule and unflustered in the very heart of Jerez de la Frontera. We even managed to park next to our hotel. The Casa Grande looked regal and elegant. Adorned with balconies, enclosed by intricately patterned railings, the whitewashed building is a restored 19th-century '*casa señorial*' – the house had originally been owned by a wine merchant who ran a bodega in the city. The outside of the hotel held the promise of sumptuous, cultivated comfort. The interior of the hotel delivered on all fronts. Tastefully appointed, cool and spacious rooms surrounded an open central courtyard, where you could take breakfast or indulge in a drink. The tiled courtyard was framed by six columns that supported the balustraded upper floors. Will and Tom had a room on the ground floor, but Tania and I climbed higher. Situated on the second floor we were able to gaze out and watch the world go by from our own private balcony. The three-storey hotel was topped off by a large and delightful roof terrace, which also housed a smaller, higher terrace, with room for just two. This crowning glory, accessed by a steep, spiral staircase, provided peace, privacy and spectacular city views.

The proprietress of the hotel was both friendly and charming; Spanish through and through, she spoke perfect English, with BBC-style Received Pronunciation – an accent, or perhaps a lack of any accent, identified by social class rather than by region. After proudly showing us around Casa Grande, she gave us directions so that we wouldn't miss our afternoon rendezvous with Gonzalez Byass; she also recommended some authentic eateries and flamenco bars for later in the evening.

Our afternoon rendezvous was linked to Jerez de la Frontera's most famous product. Jerez de la Frontera is synonymous with wine making, and quite literally so. Early English travellers enjoyed the fortified wine that Jerez had to offer, but either because of poor pronunciation or possibly over indulgence, the word 'Jerez', from the Moorish 'Sherish', was corrupted to become 'Sherry'. Sherry now has protected origin status within Europe. All wine labelled as sherry must come from an area between Jerez de la Frontera, Sanlucar de Barrameda and El Puerto de Santa Maria.

Sherry is made from white grapes, primarily the Palomino grape. Types of sherry range from the light but dry Manzanilla and Fino, to the darker and heavier Amontillado and Oloroso. Tania's favourite, Pedro Ximenez, is a sweet, dark, dessert sherry. Wine making in the area around Jerez de la Frontera goes back to the Phoenicians and the Romans; perhaps somewhat surprisingly, production continued under Arab rule. Things really took off, however, after the Reconquista. By the 16th century, Jerez de la Frontera was reputed to be producing the finest wines in the world. This global reputation was enhanced by piracy and plunder.

In 1597, Sir Francis Drake sacked Cadiz, stealing 2,900 barrels of sherry in the process. Shipped back to England, the English were soon hooked on sherry; piracy and plunder turned into profit and trade. Sherry was so popular and profitable that many English entrepreneurs invested in the wine and sherry making business. One such entrepreneur was Mr Byass, who joined forces with Señor Manuel Marie Gonzalez Angel; a dynasty was born. Gonzalez Byass is now one of the most famous sherry bodegas (or wineries) in the world. Our appointment with Gonzalez Byass was a pre-booked sherry tasting and tapas tour.

Situated beside a grand Gothic cathedral, the home of Gonzalez Byass looked to have been built on a similarly impressive scale and appeared to demand a similar level of reverence. Speaking in hushed tones, we entered and admired the main building, before looking at pictures of famous and infamous previous visitors: the present merged with the past as an image of Margaret Thatcher threatened to ruin my tour before it had even begun. Turning to the left, always the left, we joined a multinational tour group and met our designated guide. After a brief introduction, we were ushered into another room and shown a film about the history of the company, which was actually much more interesting than it sounds. After the film, we toured the bodega in a small train, which stopped at various points along the way. Our first stop was an impressive round building, designed by none other than Gustav Eiffel, he of the eponymous tower. The building contained 120 barrels, each marked with the coat of arms of different countries from around the world. After taking a few photos, we moved to another building where our guide explained how sherry is made. The local climate and chalky soils around Jerez de la Frontera create a local sherry wine, which is fortified with grape juice before being transferred to oak barrels. Loose stoppers let in air and a layer of 'flor' or yeast develops on the surface of the wine. This layer prevents oxidisation and feeds off the wine at the same time. Apparently, it's the subtle nature of the 'flor' that accounts for the unique flavour of Jerez sherry; but that's not the end of the process. The wine is fortified with alcohol and then blended with older wines over a period of time in what is known as the Solera system. The classic final product is the bone dry Fino, but if the 'flor' is allowed to die in the barrel you end up with a slightly nutty Amontillado; allow the alcohol content to increase and restrict the development of the 'flor' and you have an Oloroso; add sweet grapes and cream and you have a classic pale cream sherry – 'Crofts Original' to be precise.

Taste buds tantalised, but not yet satisfied, we hopped back on the train and continued our tour. We began to get a real sense of the scale of the place, which resembled a small town. We passed beautiful gardens, streets lined with red geraniums, streets lined with vines, numerous bodegas, a museum and the 'Tio Pepe' Steps. Tio Pepe, the world's bestselling Fino, was named after Manuel Maria Gonzalez Angel's 'Uncle Joe', who created the drink in 1841. Our next stop was the Bodega La Constancia. This entire bodega is dedicated to the ageing of Tio Pepe. '*La Constancia*' (constancy) was the motto of the founder of the company and it was the first bodega to be constructed in 1855. We enjoyed looking at the huge rows of casks, many of which had been signed by the rich, famous and not so famous – Bobby Charlton, Roger Moore, Picasso, Orson Wells, Oliver Hardy, Michael Portillo, Javier Bardem and Franco (although we didn't see his particular cask) had all left their mark.

Our tour ended in the Gran Bodega. Under one of the four immense concrete domes that enclose the building, we were finally able to sample the produce and satisfy our taste buds. We were given some tasty tapas and offered four different types of sherry (all of us, that is, apart from Tom). I had to agree with Tania, the Pedro Ximenez reigned supreme.

After a brief return to Casa Grande, for a quick siesta, we heeded the owner's advice and headed out hoping to discover some authenticity. The genuine article that we were hoping to discover was good food and drink at good prices, followed by some real flamenco in a real Spanish bar.

Our first destination was a lively tapas restaurant located in a pedestrianised square opposite the town hall. On first inspection, Albores looked to be a little bit too modern for our taste, but it was full of customers and they all appeared to be Spanish. On second inspection, our doubts proved to be unfounded; the food was simply delicious and very much to our taste. All the food that we ordered was of the finest quality and all the plates were presented as if they were works of art. The food that we didn't order was also delightful. Seconds after ordering *pulpo en tempura*, our waiter arrived with a plate of '*croquetas*'. '*Pulpo?*' I asked quizzically. '*Si señor*,' he confirmed. Ten minutes later, after consuming what turned out to be someone else's prawn, spinach and pistachio *croquetas*, our actual order arrived. The *croquetas* were excellent, but our favourite dishes were the originally ordered *pulpo en tempura con patatas* (octopus in tempura batter with a creamy potato and garlic sauce) and the *morcilla artesanna de*

Burgos con compote de manzana (black pudding with an apple compote). Both dishes exemplified all that is best about Spanish cuisine; the food was good enough to rival the quite magnificent Barrafina in London.

Our second destination was supposedly just the place to discover real flamenco. The small bar certainly looked authentic enough: old and slightly rundown, the faded and stained whitewashed exterior, with its green-tiled Art Deco styled signage, looked basic but brilliant. Tabanco el Pasaje opened onto two different streets, and a long wooden, wine-soaked counter stretched from door to door. Apart from the immediate area next to both doorways, the bar was completely packed. Stepping inside was like stepping into a different world; you could sense the passion and you could feel the heat. Our senses began to work overtime. We could hear the shill notes and the wailing of a flamenco singer, accompanied by the rapid finger plucking of a guitarist, but we couldn't see either performer. We could feel the pressure of the crowd and taste the excitement. Pushing and squeezing our way through the crowd, muttering '*perdon*' from time to time, we reached a point where if we stood on tiptoes we could see both performers. Hemmed in to one corner of a recessed area of the bar, a dark-haired, emotionally charged, beautiful singer in an elegant yellow dress appeared to be united in the moment with both her guitarist and the audience. Lost somewhere between heaven and earth, the audience silently followed each and every note that was sung or played. Deeply engrossed and fully absorbed, this collective concentration and adoration was sometimes broken by moments of spontaneous shouting, screaming and clapping, as one individual performance gave way to another. You could almost taste the *duende*. Forget about the touristic 'meal and a show' sanitised, germ-free theatrical flamenco, this was the real thing – genuine, original, bona fide and fully authentic. I'd fallen in love with flamenco.

The origins of flamenco are shrouded in mystery, but perceived wisdom appears to suggest that it was born out of the fusion of Gypsy or Gitano (the Romani people of Spain) and Moriscos culture. The origin of the word *flamenco* is also uncertain; it may have been derived from 'fire' or 'flame', but it may have come from the Hispanic-Arabic term *fellas mengu*, which means 'expelled peasant'. What is without doubt is the fact that flamenco originated in Andalusia, and Andalusia was a cultural melting pot. When the Moriscos were expelled from Andalusia, many avoided persecution by fleeing to live with the

Gitanos, who lived on the fringes of society. The different cultures, with their eastern past and their western present, developed a unique style of singing. In its original form, flamenco was all about the voice. An almost primitive cry or chant would have been accompanied by a rhythmic hand clap or foot stamp. This unspoilt vocal style is known as *Cante jondo*, which means 'deep music'. The guitar was introduced at a later date. Lorca described *Cante jondo* as 'the rhythm of birds and the natural music of the black poplar and the waves; it is simple in oldness and style. It is also a rare example of primitive song, the oldest of all Europe, where the ruins of history, the lyrical fragment eaten by the sand, appear live like the first morning of life.' The flamenco in Tabanco el Pasaje was certainly deep music; it entered through your ears and eyes, and then it enveloped your soul. Lorca associated flamenco with *duende*, but stated that 'duende could only be present when one sensed that death was possible'. For me, the joy of our flamenco experience, and indeed the joy of Spain, is that the music and the country make you feel alive – animated, vibrant and vital.

If the music wasn't enough for anyone, Tabanco el Pasaje also offered amazingly cheap drinks: one euro for a wine or a beer – admittedly the fino tasted like paint stripper, but the rough red wine fitted the moment. We listened to the rest of the flamenco performance, sipping our drinks and feeding off the atmosphere. A particularly thunderous round of applause signalled the end of the performance and the departure of the singer. Walking out through the in door, the singer was treated like a superstar. Mobbed by men, women and children alike, she posed for photographs and autographed just about anything and everything that came to hand.

Reflecting on the evening, I realised that I hadn't just fallen in love with flamenco, but also with Tabanco el Pasaje and Jerez de la Frontera. I could happily have stayed in the bar all night long and the city was a revelation. The size and the scale of Jerez de la Frontera wasn't too daunting (we could easily find our way around) but the city housed many grand buildings, and even in the height of summer (or perhaps *because* it was the height of summer) there weren't too many tourists. We concluded our night away with drinks on the hotel roof terrace, followed in the morning by a breakfast of coffee and churros and a trip to the cathedral.

Rather appropriately, we left Jerez de la Frontera to the sound of silence; nothing could have lived up to the sound of the night before.

IN-BETWEEN DAYS

THIS IS NOW

Casa Mesto, our home from home, was an isolated, restored farmstead, located amongst 'Los Pueblos Blancos', the white villages of Andalusia. Every year, once the spring rains have passed, the houses of 'Los Pueblos Blancos' are whitewashed to a state of pristine perfection, partly as a way of welcoming the new season and saying a final *adiós* to the colder winter months, and partly – and less romantically – as a way of carrying out general maintenance. Almost whiter than white, the houses reflect the sun and dazzle in contrast to the sombre rocky backdrop of the sierras. Famous and fantastic, 'Los Pueblos Blancos' are renowned for their unique beauty and their spectacular mountain settings. Influenced by the Berber architecture of North Africa, the small villages and towns are invariably located on hilltops; the whitewashed houses huddle around ancient castles and churches, creating captivating built landscapes which rival the work of nature.

Although located amongst 'Los Pueblos Blancos', Casa Mesto is situated between one 'Pueblo Blanco' and one 'Pueblo Azul'. Confused? So were we. Casa Mesto is situated between Juzcar to the south and Cartijima to the north. Juzcar, about a twenty-minute walk from our front door, used to be one of the 'Pueblo Blancos', but in 2011 all the buildings in the village (including the church and the gravestones) were painted blue by Sony Pictures to promote the launch of a new 3D *Smurfs* movie and to celebrate 'Global Smurfs Day' – who would have thought that such a day even existed? We had been informed about this tinted travesty in advance of our visit to the village, but nothing could have quite prepared us for the spectacle – Juzcar really does stand out. Positioned somewhere on a colour chart between sky blue and electric blue, 'Smurf' blue is out there on its own – quite literally so, as the colour has now been trademarked. To my mind (and Will's) the colour jarred against the natural landscape, but Tania and Tom, and most of the local villagers, were in favour of the redecoration. Sony offered to repaint the town after the main event, but the locals voted to extend Juzcar's blue period. This vote has been justified by the fact that since turning blue, the village's finances have moved from the red

into the black. Tourists numbers have leapt from 300 visitors a year to over 250 visitors a day; several small new businesses have opened and profits have grown.

With a mixed sense of alarm, interest and admiration (well, as publicity stunts go it has been a pretty successful one) we explored the village. Wandering around, we gazed in mild amusement at the many pictures of Smurfs and

Smurfettes painted onto the sides of houses. We walked past models of Smurfs, Smurfettes and their toadstool homes, but we resisted the temptation to stop or step inside. Mostly bizarre, some of the models were even more bizarre than others. We stared in frank astonishment at a line of disembodied Smurf heads which had been raised high on poles on top of a balcony; the scene resembled the aftermath of a medieval massacre. Emotionally disturbed, we visited the village shop in search of some cooling, and hopefully calming, water. Unfortunately, the shop stocked little in the way of basic necessities; however, it did sell a comprehensive range of Smurf merchandise and memorabilia. Heading onwards, we visited the local bar. Apart from some red chairs and a green awning, Bar Torricheli was blue inside and out. Cheap, lively and friendly, with good food and drink, the bar was a little gem. Tania and I enjoyed a beer, but we noticed that most of the locals were drinking a pink-coloured drink served with lots of ice. Determined to follow our own advice, which is to eat and drink as the locals do, we tried some 'Pacharan'. The sweet liqueur wine was delicious and fairly potent. Originally produced in Navarre, Pacharan is made from fermented sloes and has an alcohol content of between 25 and 30 per cent. A couple of glasses later and the village of Juzcar began to feel a little less bizarre. A couple more glasses and I thought I was hallucinating. Fortunately, the boys were able to guide us home.

We have generally found that when we are on holiday with the boys, it's a good idea to alternate busy days with rest days. Some days are packed full of cities, sights, museums, shops and social history, but on other days we just read, swim, rest, relax and laze about. Our 'full-on' days are usually separated by 'in-between days'; I think it's the secret to a happy holiday. Our evening trip to Juzcar had been tagged onto a lazy day, which had followed our frantic and full-on trip to Jerez de la Frontera. Too much Pacharan, however, meant that one in-between day was about to become two.

After a later breakfast than usual, we decided to rest up and enjoy all that our holiday home had to offer. After all, if you can't relax and do just what you want to do when you are on holiday, when can you? To some extent our plan was determined by our post-Pacharan performance, but it was our last full day at Casa Mesto, and I for one was more than happy to spend the day doing nothing.

A rest cure was obviously what was required. My head began to clear, so I took a break from doing nothing and headed towards the infinity pool. As

I wallowed in the cool blue water and gazed towards the Sierra Bermeja, I realised that this was another of those perfect moments. I looked across the garden and saw William and Tom, laughing and smiling as they chatted, whilst Tania immersed herself in a book. The cicadas chirruped, a gentle breeze blew and the sun shone. What could be better or more life-affirming? I was a happy, proud and contented man.

Unfortunately, all good things come to an end. Tania finished her book and suggested that as this was our last day, we should probably get rid of all the waste and rubbish that we had accumulated during our short stay – this included a few too many empty bottles and cans. Resistance was useless, contentment was curtailed. The nearest bottle bank was in Cartijima, I would have to venture out after all. I asked for volunteers to accompany me, but eye contact was avoided and silence reigned supreme. Teenage volunteers were in short supply, but Tania did agree to help.

As local recycling centres go, Cartijima was a particularly impressive one. The village occupies a quite spectacular physical space. Perched above an oak forest, the village is surmounted by rugged limestone peaks. The village possesses all the traditional characteristics of a Pueblo Blanco: narrow streets and immaculate white houses, tightly clustered around an ancient church. Apart from the immediate area next to the recycling bins, the village was archetypal and attractive.

Our intention, as we parked on the outskirts of the village, was to quickly carry out our chores and then return to base. However, we were seduced by Cartijima's charms and intrigued by the faint sound of distant voices.

Intrigued and entranced, we headed towards what we presumed would be the centre of the village, but finding our way was difficult. The maze-like arrangement of the alleyways and streets proved to be quite disorientating; it was impossible to head in a straight line. By continually reacting and redirecting to the growing noise we attempted to keep on course. Sound was our compass, and as the decibels grew we became even more intrigued. What had at first been a murmur, a distant gabble, slowly and almost imperceptibly rose to a crescendo. As we got closer to the centre of the action we heard individual shouts and shrieks ringing out above what sounded like the collective chant of a football crowd. Cartijima, a small village of just over 200 residents, sounded like it had been invaded.

Turning a final corner, we arrived at a busy and bustling square. With a stage at one end and a bar at the other, practically the whole village, plus a few guests, were either sitting down and talking or standing around and talking. Those who were seated sat beside rows of tables that packed the space between stage and bar; those standing ordered drinks and ate tapas. Voices amplified by friendly, but competitive, conversation were further amplified by the surrounding architectural acoustics. Everyone appeared to have something to say and everyone wanted to make themselves heard. Young and old talked and mixed freely, but some behavioural and spatial patterns did exist. The older women generally sat close to the stage, fanning themselves as they drank, talked, ate and fussed over their grandchildren. The older men on the edge of the throng talked, drank, smoked, played cards and reminisced. Mothers and fathers stood close to the bar, enjoying quality time with each other as they remembered that they had once been 'novias' and 'novios', whilst teenagers flirted and engaged in games almost as old as time. Amidst the scene, young children ran around freely, indulged by all they were blithely unencumbered by North European convention. I got the distinct impression that this was a happy place and a safe place; a place where everyone would look out for everyone else; a place where it would be impossible to die alone or uncared about. Cartijima, at least for today, was a model for life as it's meant to be lived.

Feeling like a pair of uninvited guests at a party, we hesitated, not knowing quite what to do. We didn't think that we should gate-crash, but we were beckoned towards the bar by friendly faces and invited to eat and drink along with everyone else. Having failed to learn any lessons from our Pacharan experience, we decided to drink what the locals were drinking. Pointing at a tall glass full of red-tinted promise and asking 'Qué es?', I was informed that the drink in question was *tinto de verano*, or 'red wine of summer'. The drink turned out to be a simple, but delightful mixture of red wine and *gaseosa* (a mild flavoured lemonade) served with lots of ice. The drink hit the spot nicely; it was the perfect accompaniment to the mood and to the moment. The food was equally as delightful as the drink. A constant stream of delicious treats were delivered to the bar and to the tables: stuffed peppers, cheese, Iberico ham, tuna, potato and pork fillets. Perfect strangers pushed plates heaped with food towards us. We were outsiders, but we were treated like old friends. The drinks only cost a euro and all the food was free. This was a village that wanted to share itself and its produce. Living as we do in an age of semi-isolation, self-interest and selfism, the whole experience was uniquely satisfying. Loud, passionate, warm, welcoming, communal, caring and carefree, Catijima exemplified all that is best about village life in Spain.

We had been fortunate enough to arrive on one of three summer festival days. On 14, 15 and 16 August, food was provided free of charge to all who visited Cartijima. We had arrived on the barbecued meats day, but on the day before a giant paella cooked in a giant pan had been served to all and sundry; on the day after our visit, a feast of sardines would be provided. The three-day *feria* is preceded by a cultural week. Theatre, music and dancing dominate life in the village. *Feria* (Latin for 'free day') was originally used to describe a day on which slaves were not obliged to work; now it means a fair or festival, but fair days are still public holidays. The Cartijima *feria* is reputed to be the best in the area. The nature of Cartijima's *feria* and its local pre-eminence is due in part to the village's recent history.

Franco died in 1975, but it would take another thirty-two years for Cartijima to shake off his influence. In 2007, the villagers finally overcame their collective inferiority complex and felt confident enough to freely exercise their democratic rights and vote out the incumbent Francoist mayor. The largely uneducated and illiterate population had found it difficult to break away from years of suppression and coercion. The new mayor created a new dynamism and opened up the town hall and its kitchens to everyone. Free from intimidation, the villagers partied into the night – they're still partying. The Cartijima *feria* is an outward expression of recently won freedom.

When you become a parent you voluntarily give up freedom, but would I be without my children? Well, not most of the time. It has always struck me as strange that we give up so easily what little we have to lose. After eating and drinking our fill we thought that it was probably time to re-engage with our parental responsibilities, so we headed back to Casa Mesto. We were slightly worried that the boys would have been wondering what had happened to us, but it was evident that they hadn't even really registered that we had gone in the first place. They may not have noticed our earlier departure, but when we mentioned free food and stated our intention to return and visit the *feria* by night, they stated their intention to accompany us.

Later that evening we parked in the same spot that we had used earlier in the day. This time, however, the sound of distant voices was replaced by the sound of a sudden, sharp and loud explosion. Jumping, despite ourselves and our better instincts, we looked up towards the sky. It was still daytime, but a spider's web of fluorescent white light radiated from a central point of brilliance. The bright light soon faded, outlasted by the boom of the blast echoing around the hillsides, diminishing with each reverberation. Peace was all but restored, but then another explosion rent the sky and the pattern was repeated. We should have been more prepared for the second blast, but we still jumped.

We were obviously watching and listening to fireworks, but these weren't like any fireworks that I had ever seen or heard before. These were more like military rockets, launched singularly and with dramatic effect. We discovered later that many of the rockets were lit whilst still being held, fuses ignited with the help of glowing cigarette tips. Children would then race around the village, competing to catch the stabilising sticks that the rockets had originally been attached to as they fell back down to earth. Health and safety regulations appear to have bypassed Cartijima.

As our ears and then our nerves slowly recovered, we picked out the sound of distant drums and what we thought was possibly a brass section. Once again, directed by sound, we headed back towards the centre of the village, but this time the village came out to meet us. We hadn't walked far before the drumming became louder, the sound of brass became unmistakable and the streets become crowded with people. The young, the old, and people of indeterminate age hugged pavements and doorways, leaving a narrow processional avenue for players, parishioners, prelates and a *paso*. The *paso*, an elaborate float carried by six porters, was finished in silver and gold and was surmounted by a statue of the Madonna and Child. The life-size and lifelike figures were dressed in green and gold, and they were adorned with pink roses. Some of the instrumentalists formed a guard of honour surrounding the float; others followed on behind, as did many of the villagers. Squeezing ourselves tightly against the ancient walls of ancient houses, we felt like we had stepped back in time. The procession moved slowly, the hesitant and somewhat stilted movements had obviously been reverently and lovingly choreographed – it was an extraordinary and intriguingly emotional sight. Spain is a modern country with modern ambitions, but its soul is rooted deeply and firmly in the past.

Returning to the present, we followed the procession as it wound its way through the village and back to the church. The interior of Nuestra Señora del Rosario (Our Lady of the Rosary) owes far more to recent times than does the ancient exterior of the building. Restored after being set ablaze, the original interior of the church was an early victim of the Spanish Civil War.

This was the penultimate day of the *feria*, but the first day is always dedicated to women – those who live in the village and those who left during and just after the Civil War, but who return to their spiritual home in August. I felt like I had discovered my spiritual home. Returning to the square, we lost ourselves in the warm embrace of Cartijima. We were welcomed with open arms, full plates, music, dancing and drink. We felt like – and we were made to feel like – we belonged. Here, I thought, is a culture and a way of life that can be believed in.

That Was Then

When you're young, anything and everything seems possible; doubt may be an overriding emotion, but doubt doesn't dent possibility.

My father was a musical man. He was an accomplished pianist and had played in a number of jazz bands. Impressively, he could hear a tune on the radio one minute and play it the next. From an early age I was a little in awe of my father's musical ability, but I chose to learn the guitar rather than the piano. It quickly became apparent, however, that whilst I could play at a fairly rudimentary level (entertaining myself, but no one else) I was never going to be booked to perform at the Royal Albert Hall.

I probably would have given up the guitar, but then I saw Louise.

Our eyes first met (well, mine met hers) across the aisles of the local Roman Catholic church. Louise sat playing her guitar at the front of the church: she was pretty, she was perfection, she was a member of the folk group and she was my first real crush. I should have realised that she was unobtainable, but I was 13 and hormonal. Against my own better judgement and in the absence of wisdom, I hatched a cunning plan. Approaching the leader of the folk group, I volunteered my services. I became a fully signed-up member of the musical ensemble and I knew that my chance would come.

Louise left the group the very next week – perhaps this was not an unconnected fact.

Unfortunately, when I attempted to leave the group, my father told me that I had made a commitment and commitments had to be honoured. I was destined to spend every other Sunday for the next two years strumming along to 'Lord of the Dance' and 'Michael, Row the Boat Ashore' – Hallelujah indeed.

From those days to these, I have never played either song again, but my salutary experience would come in useful in Granada.

During the week, Ariana and her flatmate Alison spent mornings and sometimes afternoons at the university. Left to my own devices, I read, slept, sunbathed, explored the city and strummed away on an old guitar that I had discovered in the flat. My idle strumming gave birth to an idea.

I still had grave doubts about my guitar playing ability and deep down I knew that I couldn't really sing, but I believed that I might be able to supplement my meagre finances by busking, and I wasn't going to let the fact that I only knew four chords and three and half songs get in the way.

Reciting lyrics and picturing chord sequences, I headed out early one morning into the city streets of Granada. My challenge to myself was to earn enough money to pay for breakfast. Guitar in hand, I searched for a quiet spot in a local square. Doubts crowded my mind; the possible suddenly and overwhelmingly seemed impossible. 'It's now or never,' I thought to myself. Trying to disregard everyone else and just play for myself, I formed a G chord and then an E minor, but I couldn't make myself strum the strings. My hands sweated, despite the cool of morning. Wiping my hands on my jeans, I went back to G again. This time I managed to make a sound, but it was so quiet that no one apart from myself could possibly have heard it. I struggled on. I accompanied my own hushed chords with whispered incoherent words. 'Police car and a screaming siren, pneumatic drill and ripped up concrete.' It was a performance of sorts, but it wasn't entertainment. I put the guitar down and searched for inspiration.

I hadn't earned enough for breakfast (I hadn't earned enough for anything) but I needed a drink and I didn't think an orange juice would do. Ordering a *sol y sombra*, with a coffee on the side, I tried to resurrect my confidence. *Sol y sombra*, or 'sun and shade', consists of equal measures of brandy and anise. The drink, usually served as a digestif, is sometimes drunk to kickstart the day. I contemplated the day ahead and hoped that a little Dutch courage would do the trick. Friends, or more accurately acquaintances in the bar, were intrigued to see that I had a guitar with me. From odd words, gestures and signs, I gathered that they wanted me to play. Fuelled by early morning *sol*, and some *sombra*, I played, but didn't sing. My musicianship was greeted with polite applause and a pat on the back. Perhaps I wasn't that bad after all? Perhaps it was the drink talking? Perhaps they were just being kind? Whatever the real reasons, my confidence grew and my inhibitions fell.

Somewhat surprisingly, someone in the bar rewarded my playing with the offer of another drink. '*Un otro*,' I said. Too much sun is bad for everyone, but a little *sol*, tempered with some shade, perked me up no end. It was time to go on tour. Consigning my first busking experience to history, I boarded a bus and headed towards the Albaicin. Doubt had been replaced by belief.

With a new sense of casual self-assurance, I decided to follow the Calle San Juan de Los Reyes, and play at likely spots along the route. My performances were necessarily, and from the point of view of the public, fortuitously brief: three and a half songs didn't make for a long show. Powered by brandy and anise, I thought I sounded great. 'That's Entertainment' by The Jam, 'Bank Robber' by The Clash, 'The Boxer' by Simon and Garfunkel, and half of 'Still Ill' by The Smiths, were reeled off in quick succession. I tried to sound as impassioned as Paul Weller, I thought I was Joe Strummer and I wanted to be Morrissey. I was tempted to play more, but after four separate performances a string broke and the people of Granada were spared.

Heading onwards rather than heading home, I continued to follow the Calle San Juan de Los Reyes and then detoured towards the Mirador San Nicolas. Perched on a wall opposite San Nicolas Church, against the stunning backdrop of the Alhambra, two guitarists were mid-performance. The dexterity of their playing, the quality of their musicianship, the passion in their voices and their fingertips, made all my efforts seem shabbily mediocre. I watched and listened, enthralled. I loved the moment, I loved the show, but my own self-assurance dissipated as belief was replaced by doubt. I had rediscovered reality and I had only earned a few pesetas, but I had proved to myself that anything is possible if you have a go. I looked at my broken guitar string with a sense of thankfulness: at least no one could ask or expect me to play.

OUT OF ADVERSITY
Nerja and the Basque Country

THIS IS NOW

'Out of adversity comes opportunity', or so some people say. If you ask me, adversity is overrated, but it's undeniably true that experiencing bad times can lead to good times. Experiencing bad times also heightens our enjoyment of the good times. That euphoric Friday feeling just wouldn't be the same without the misery of a Monday morning.

We weren't miserable and it wasn't Monday morning – it was a sunny Saturday. Although we were a little sad to be leaving Casa Mesto, after such a fantastic week, our sadness was more than compensated for by the excitement of heading somewhere new. Guidebooks suggested that Nerja had some fine beaches and was relatively unspoilt. We headed south, blissfully unaware of the embryonic shadows cast by our optimism.

The drive was scenic and fortunately uneventful. After stopping to buy some groceries in a shopping mall on the outskirts of Malaga, we arrived in Nerja. I suppose 'relatively unspoilt' is a subjective term, but first impressions were not favourable. Admittedly, we had been spoilt by our unspoilt mountainous retreat, but Nerja looked far from fine. Apartments, tower blocks and concrete dominated the scene. With a growing sense of pessimism, we passed restaurants, cafes and bars advertising pints of beer and full English breakfasts, as we headed towards the Hotel Club Nerja. We weren't staying in the hotel, but it was from here that we needed to collect the keys for our apartment which had been booked through Owners Direct. Owners Direct specialises in advertising privately owned properties, which are then booked directly from the owners. We have used the company on several occasions and up until Nerja, we had never been disappointed.

I suppose there has to be a first time for everything.

Arriving at the hotel, we were told that there weren't any keys to collect. My first thought was that either the apartment or the owner didn't actually exist, but after a fairly fraught conversation with the hotel receptionist, it became apparent that the keys, which had been left in our name, had already been collected, about an hour before we had arrived. 'A little strange,' I thought to myself. Maybe a cleaner was giving the flat a final once-over? Unable to contact the owner of the property, we decided to visit the apartment and find out for ourselves.

The apartment was located in a block of flats, which was only a short distance from the hotel, but we managed to turn a short walk into a long one. Wrong turns dominated proceedings. The block of flats, when we eventually arrived, was not what we had expected. Located next to an unfinished building (a concrete skeleton of quite impressive ugliness) the block blended in well with its surroundings, but the surroundings resembled the worst of Eastern Bloc architectural development. We walked past a communal swimming pool, but everything about it argued against communality. The pool was small, too small to swim in, and it was surrounded by plastic grass. A teenage couple looked to be in danger of drowning in their own saliva as they embraced and frolicked in the shallows. I hoped that the chlorine levels were high. An English family sat by the edge of the pool – F-words filled the air, smoke billowed from cigarettes and faded tattoos were embraced by folds of fat, and that was just the children.

Lazy sunbathers without a care in the world. Come on in, the water's lovely!

'Where's number 14?' I said, to everyone and no one in particularly. Ears pricked up, and out of the corner of my eye I glimpsed the lazy sunbathers stirring – wary glances began to track our movements. We located the apartment and knocked, but there was no reply. Standing outside number 14, we were homeless and increasingly humourless. The area and the apartment may not have been exactly what we wanted, but we needed somewhere to stay. As we discussed our next move, I heard footsteps approaching. Turning, I was confronted by a pot-bellied, pasty person wearing speedos that were several sizes too small for him – the phony war was over.

'What d'ya want,' he asked.

I explained our position. 'I don't know if you can help us? We've booked number 14, but the keys have been collected by someone else and we're trying to find out what's going on.' The man looked confused and guilty at the same time. 'We're staying here,' he offered by way of explanation. 'Oh, I see,' I said. 'Well, I think there's been some kind of mistake, because we're booked to stay here this week and the keys left at the hotel were left in our name.' Tania showed him electronic confirmation of the facts to clarify our position. Speedo man looked and then looked away again. He was clearly concerned, but he was clearly unwilling to discuss the situation any further. 'Have you got any proof of booking?' I asked. 'An email or a letter?' Ignoring me, the man called his wife. They unlocked the door, stepped inside and slammed the door shut. 'I'll take that as a no then,' I shouted as they disappeared.

I knocked again, more in hope than expectation. The door remained stubbornly and firmly closed. Silence reigned supreme. Supreme, that is, until silence was broken by the sound of The Smiths – my phone was ringing.

Our many efforts to get in contact with the owner of the property via texts, phone calls and emails had finally paid off. David, the owner, could usually be found in Spain, but he was ringing from Ireland. 'Don't worry,' he said. 'I'll sort everything out,' he said. 'The apartment is yours,' he said. David told us that the other family shouldn't have been in the property. He informed us that they had booked to stay for the preceding week. He was calm and reassuring, and he sounded genuinely upset and concerned on our behalf. However, we didn't feel as confident as David sounded. The other family had possession of the apartment and it didn't look like they were going to move out anytime soon.

It was also difficult to see how they could have booked flights, taken time off work and flown to Spain, for the wrong week. To be fair to the other family, it's no wonder they looked baffled, but they could at least have attempted to be helpful and they shouldn't have picked up keys that were clearly being held for us. We reserved our sympathy for ourselves.

We returned to the Hotel Club Nerja, grabbed a much-needed drink and waited. Every twenty minutes or so, David phoned to tell us that everything would be fine, but as the phone calls and the minutes passed we grew increasingly concerned. After telling us not to worry for what seemed like the twenty-seventh time, David confirmed that after checking all his email accounts, he had managed to double-book the apartment. We didn't know whether to laugh or cry – I think we did both. David said that he would find us something else, but we were losing faith in him and in Nerja.

Not only were we losing faith, but we were running out of time. We needed a room for the night, and we also wanted to try and save some of the food that we had brought with us, which by now must have been slowly cooking in the car. Taking all things into consideration, we decided to book a hotel. Unfortunately, there didn't appear to be any rooms at any of the inns. It was the first Saturday after the Feast of the Assumption, and everywhere we tried was full. After contacting just about every hotel in Nerja, we discovered that the only place with any availability was the Parador de Nerja, but in this case availability was a subjective term – it wasn't available to our pockets. Paradores are luxury hotels, located in castles, palaces, fortresses, convents, monasteries and modern designer-built buildings. The enterprise was founded by Alfonso XIII of Spain, as a means of promoting tourism and preserving historic buildings. Today, the Paradores are a profitable, state-run business, but even in our present predicament, the Parador de Nerja was out of our price range. Ruling out ultimate luxury, we increased our budget by as much as we dared and tried to find hotels or apartments in other areas, but all our efforts were to no avail. We sank into a state of collective despondency. It was then that I remembered Grahame.

Several years ago, Grahame, a friend and former colleague, had retired to Spain. He successfully avoided the expat Costa Geriatrica, by buying some land and building his own house in Chite, a small village to the south of Granada. In point of fact, Grahame had been the driving force behind the development of a small urbanisation, a whole new street which originally incorporated six separate plots. I clearly remember the original plans, because we were offered the chance to buy into the scheme. Unfortunately for us, the timing was all wrong. With two young children and little cash, it seemed to be an impossible dream. Looking back with the benefit of hindsight, I think we made the wrong decision. We should have begged, borrowed or stolen. I view it as a missed opportunity.

Not wanting to miss out on any more opportunities, I gave Grahame a call. I knew that he was back in the UK for the summer and I thought that his Spanish house was occupied by his family and friends, but I hoped and prayed that he might he be able to help us.

My faith was well placed.

One phone call later and we had the number of a friend of Grahame's who rented out rooms in Chite. Another phone call and we had sealed the deal. In a matter of moments, we moved from despondency to delight, and things were about to get even better.

David phoned to inform us that he still couldn't find any accommodation, but before I could tell him about our new plans, he offered to put us up in a hotel for the night. In theory we could have travelled straight to Chite, but it was late and I was tired and I'd never stayed in a Parador. I told David that the only hotel with any availability was the Parador de Nerja. The line went quiet for a moment, but then David agreed to pay. 'We'll need two rooms,' I said. Well, he owed us one.

If you don't ask, you don't get. David agreed to pay for both rooms, but payment wasn't straightforward. For reasons unknown, David told us that he had reserved the rooms, but he couldn't pay the full amount by card. To complete the transaction, David said that he would arrange for a friend of his to meet us at the hotel with a bundle of cash. Doubts resurfaced and my faith started to wane once again. Feeling anxious, we headed towards the hotel.

If truth be told, the outside of the hotel, which resembled a series of austere prison blocks, was a little disappointing, but the bright and opulent interior was quite fantastic. By now we were all really looking forward to our stay, so I hoped that everything would work out. Reporting to reception, I was relieved to discover that our rooms had been reserved. I was even more relieved when a dishevelled, slightly suspicious-looking character arrived carrying a large brown envelope – the cash had arrived. Our check-in may have resembled a dodgy drugs deal, but we were delighted to have a room that we could call our own – it was time to unpack the groceries.

Trying to fit a week's worth of shopping into two hotel minibars is no mean task. In an attempt to reduce the bulk of the shopping, we drank and devoured as much as we could during an impromptu picnic held on our balcony. It wasn't quite the Balcon de Europa, but we had a pretty good view of the hotel's ornate planted gardens. Once we were fed and watered, we felt ready to enjoy and explore the hotel's luxurious facilities. Despite our somewhat alcoholic picnic, we enjoyed a free welcome drink at the bar before touring the extensive grounds. The gardens were filled with exotic blooms and orange trees. The lush green of the manicured and well-watered lawns contrasted with the blue of the swimming pool and the blue of the Mediterranean. The hotel, situated on a cliff overlooking the sea, had quite spectacular views, but what really excited us was the fact that the hotel had its own glass elevator to take guests down to the beach.

It could perhaps be argued that Tania, Will, Tom and I should get out more often, but for once expectation was matched by reality: we enjoyed riding the elevator to such an extent that we journeyed down, up, and down again, before finally setting foot on Playa Burriana. The beach, a mix of fine sand and pebbles, was quite attractive, but the backdrop of cafes, bars and dense low-rise development spoilt the overall character. Strolling along the foreshore, avoiding umbrellas and sun-beds, whilst dodging footballs and frisbees, I tried to picture what the scene must have looked like before the advent of mass tourism. However, despite my somewhat middle-class misgiving and pretensions, I was actually in the best of moods. The sun was shining, both literally and metaphorically. We had emerged from adversity and our early evening beach promenade paved the way for the night to come.

Heading towards the old town, we walked through a series of increasingly busy, but traditional, Spanish streets. The streets were lined with some tacky-looking gift shops, but also with some lovely-looking bars and restaurants. Nerja was beginning to reveal that it was more than just another 'Costa' on the Costa del Sol – it actually had some character. Strolling along the vibrant walkways, avoiding buskers and street-side cafes, whilst dodging pushchairs and prams, I could just about picture Nerja's ancient past.

Gradually reappraising my position, I found myself warming to Nerja, and it seemed that a lot of other people liked the place as well. With each passing step, the streets were becoming increasingly crowded. The whole area began to resemble Oxford Street on the run-up to Christmas; however, it was a little bit warmer and there weren't any carol singers – although there was a singer and she could have been called Carol. I have seldom seen busier streets: people jams were commonplace. I began to feel less surprised about the fact that practically every hotel in Nerja had had no vacancies. Some people stood and chatted, some even went against the main pedestrian flow, but the bulk of the crowd appeared to be heading in one direction – they, like us, were heading towards the 'Balcon de Europa'.

The Balcon de Europa, or 'Balcony of Europe', sealed my reappraisal of the town: it's a magnificent vantage point perched on top of a towering cliff. It was once the site of a great Moorish castle. The area was completely packed, but it still managed to retain a degree of charm. The palm-lined mirador offered sweeping panoramic views of the Mediterranean and glorious glimpses of a series of small coves and beaches that lined the rocky coastline. Several of the indented coves were wonderfully backlit by red, green and blue lights. The effect was surreal, but quite wonderful.

The Balcon de Europa acquired its name when King Alfonso XII visited Nerja after an earthquake in 1885. Large parts of the town were devastated, but the king attempted to console residents with the news that they were enjoying the best view in the whole of Europe. The monarch may well have had a point, but his view was probably scant consolation to people whose homes had been destroyed. A bronze statue of the king still stares enigmatically out to sea, testament to words and hopefully not deeds – he appears to be looking the other way.

Tearing ourselves away from the crowds, we walked through an ancient archway, down some stone steps and onto one of the small beaches. The beach was deserted. Waves broke along the shoreline, gently clattering and rattling pebbles in their swash and backwash. We weren't far away from the Balcon de Europa, but the sound of the crowd had been replaced by the sound of the sea. Moonlight illuminated the scene. We could smell the sea and the salt spray and almost taste the highly oxygenated water. Everything about the moment was delightful. The sounds, the sights, the smells, the tastes and the feel of pebbles beneath our fingertips. All five senses were assaulted in the most pleasant of ways. In theory, when we focus on our senses and consequently focus on the moment, we maximise our potential for happiness. Life is meant to be lived in the present, experienced for the reality that it can be. If the experience of the present is maximised by a full-scale assault on all five senses, the 'here and now' becomes everything and life is being lived to the full. Our present situation induced a comprehensive sensory response. The actuality of the moment became everything. Who could want for anything more?

Well, the boys apparently. Teenage stomachs rumbled, so we rejoined the masses.

Pushing through the streets we looked out for places to eat. There were so many busy looking traditional bars to choose from, that while 'Jose's Law' still held true, we used TripAdvisor to speed up and aid selection. Generally, we like to take our time, looking, exploring and selecting places for ourselves, but the boys were hungry and we wanted to visit a top tapas bar. I'm actually quite a big fan of TripAdvisor; the service has its flaws, but as long as you choose places with lots of recent positive reviews, you can't go to too far wrong. Tonight's choice would be a case in point.

Los Barriles had been awarded hundreds of excellent reviews, and when we arrived it wasn't difficult to see why. The small, intimate, rustic-looking bar was packed with locals and tourists alike, the atmosphere was terrific. We were greeted by enthusiastic staff and offered tapas with our drinks. The Rioja was delicious, as was the accompanying cheese and Serrano ham. Wine casks were used as tables, but chairs were at a premium. We stood by the tiled bar, beneath an impressive display of hanging hams, savouring the food, the drink and the moment. Taking our lead from the locals, we ordered a spicy chorizo sausage. The sausage, which you cook for yourselves, was served in a flaming ceramic pig. Much fun was had by all. Just when we thought the bar couldn't get any busier, some musicians arrived. They somehow managed to squeeze themselves into a corner, before entertaining us all.

The afternoon hadn't started well, but our evening was ending in style. Tonight was rapidly becoming one of those special nights that you know you will remember for a lifetime, and we still had our rooms in the Parador to look forward to.

The train rattled and clanked as it wound its way along the track heading into the night – we rattled and clanked in unison. Our carriage, which we had to ourselves, was illuminated by a single naked lightbulb, the connecting corridor was deserted. Surreptitiously twisting and turning in a fruitless attempt to find a position that would countenance sleep, I stared at my own reflection in the window – a hollow-eyed version of a familiar face stared back. I moved again, swivelling my shoulders, but my movements were restricted by confinement and concern. Resting her head on my lap, Ariana slept peacefully, but her tear-stained eyes paid testament to an anxious and difficult day – I didn't want to wake her.

The morning, which had started well, had ended badly. When it arrived, melancholy had arrived in moments: a phone call, a desperate message and a desperate plea. A relative of Ariana's lay seriously ill in hospital. The relative had been ill for a few days, but no one had been able to get in contact with us: we didn't have a phone, post was slow and the Internet was but a distant dream. Ariana's nearest and dearest resorted to leaving a message with the university, telling her to phone them. A family tragedy looked to be unfolding.

Travelling roughly north, we needed to cross just about the whole of the country. Forced into reversing the route of the Reconquista, at times it felt like we were heading through space and time; the names of stations evoked past glories and past infamies. Our route, which was by no means direct, saw us heading from Granada to Antequera, from Antequera to Madrid, from Madrid to Vitoria and finally from Vitoria to San Sebastian.

After a total journey time of nearly twenty-four hours we arrived in the Basque Country. I must have slept, but it certainly didn't feel like it. If I did sleep, I must have been dreaming about being awake. Stiff, tired, rattled and clanked, Ariana and I yawned, stretched, grabbed our one small holdall and headed towards the hospital. The hospital, like most hospitals on first acquaintance, appeared large and imposing, a harbinger of good news and bad. Directed towards a ward on an upper floor, we didn't know what to expect, but we certainly didn't expect to be greeted by happy smiling faces.

The Spanish wear their emotions on their sleeves. Life tends to fluctuate between extremes: it's either tragedy or good fortune, tears or smiles, deep sadness or exuberant joy. Ariana's gran was old and frail, but she was also tough and determined. Confounding her doctors, rising like Lazarus, she had refused to be beaten by an illness which until a few hours earlier had looked like it was going to win. Sitting up in her bed, she had turned a corner. Relief swept through the family in a tidal wave of emotion. In a country and an area where family is everything, family bonds had been strengthened by adversity. This was a family that had known real suffering. The normal extremes of emotion had been made more extreme by past history and circumstance. A family which had been reduced and divided by politics and war, a family which had been divided by death and distance, a family which in more ways than one, was united by blood, now euphorically embraced with a new-found optimism and joy.

Celebrations lasted well into the night. Bottles were opened, songs were sung and stories were told. Family, friends and laughter filled every corner of a small family house located in the suburbs of the city. Hospitality knew no bounds – I was welcomed with open arms. I met Ariana's uncle, who had rowed from Spain into France to escape the Francoist forces; his heroic journey, which saw him challenging tides, currents, cold and non-interventionism, had not been diminished by time. Talking with pride, tinged with sadness, he and several other members of Ariana's family still lived across the border in San Jean de Luz: a haven for former Republicans and for Basque separatists. I learnt more about Ariana's grandfather, who had printed anti-fascist leaflets during the civil war, until he was arrested, imprisoned and disappeared by the Nationalists. Informed on by one of his own, he had sacrificed everything for the cause; if he had a grave, it had never been found. The stories came thick and fast, the day turned into a family festival, a rare get together to be savoured now that fear had faded. People talked of past times and politics, food and drink, family and friends. One elderly relative or neighbour, I'm not sure which, pulled up his shirt and proudly displayed the scars of battle: a bullet wound, an indelible mark of the terror of a country which had been at war with itself. Another of Ariana's uncles, our host it transpired, took me into his back garden to see his rabbits. They happily scurried about in a run. 'Which you like?' he asked in broken English. '*El gris*,' I replied, pointing at a particularly cute rabbit who gently nibbled a carrot in wide-eyed wonderment. '*Bueno*,' my companion replied, before bending down, grabbing the rabbit and dispatching it with a speed and dexterity that defied his years. The next time I saw the rabbit, it was accompanied by white beans and chorizo.

Sharing stories, drink and food (but not rabbit), it became apparent to me that Ariana's family were bonded by love and pride; they demonstrated not only a warm and content sense of attachment towards each other, but they also exhibited a fulfilled sense of belonging to something that was greater than themselves. The Spanish are a loving and proud people, part of a proud nation, but the Basques take pride to a whole new level. The source of much of this pride is the Basque language.

Basques see themselves as the original Europeans; some of them see themselves as the direct descendants of Adam and Eve. While the latter theory seems slightly fanciful to modern minds (to say the least), the former theory has its basis in fact. The Basques are an indigenous ethnic group, characterised by their culture, a shared ancestry and most importantly of all, their language. In the Basque language, or Euskara, Basques are known as Euskaldunak, which means 'speakers of the Basque language'. The Basque language is unrelated to any other spoken language. It predates the arrival of Indo-European languages into Western Europe – it's a living relic from a bygone age. DNA research demonstrates that Basque genetic uniqueness predates the arrival of agriculture into the Iberian Peninsula, and that occurred about 7,000 years ago. Original hunter-gatherer Basques did mix with some of the early farmers, but the resultant hybrid group became isolated once again. Indigenous to and primarily inhabiting an area traditionally known as the Basque Country, a region which is located around the western end of the Pyrenees, on the coast of the Bay of Biscay, bestriding parts of north-central Spain and south-western France, the Basques are a truly unique and ancient people. It's quite possible that the Basques are the oldest continuously surviving people inhabiting a particular location in Europe.

Longevity of unique individuality and location is linked to geography. It appears that the Basques and their antecedents chose a homeland that was well suited to isolation and survival. Surrounded by mountains, dense forest and vegetation, the Basque Country was to all intents and purposes cut off from large groups of outsiders. Furthermore, the Basque lands were not highly prized: the climate was good enough to support agriculture, but the soils were not as fertile as those on the surrounding plains and the area was bereft of precious metals. On the occasions that incursions did occur, the Basques could take to the mountains and return when the coast was clear.

Little developed by the Romans, attacked, but not subdued by the Visigoths, the Normans or initially the Franks, Vasconia, as the land of the Basques was known, united with Aquitaine, to form a strong independent realm. The Basques, however, did not constitute a single political entity, but were rather a people with a certain amount of confederate organisation. Holding out fairly successfully for a number of years, Vasconia was eventually forced to submit to Frankish rule, but uprisings were a common occurrence and the Basques fought to reassert their independence. From the mid-9th century, Vasconia, renamed Navarre, grew in power and importance, taking over and controlling areas with non-Basque populations, as well as providing resistance to Moorish expansion – it could be argued that it was from Navarre that the Reconquista truly started. The influence of the Basque people reached its peak in the Middle Ages, during the reign of Sancho III, King of Navarre. At its height, the Kingdom of Navarre encompassed the entire current Basque Country in Spain (Biscay, Guipúzcoa and Álava), along with the present-day region of Navarre, the Northern Basque Country in France and parts of the Spanish provinces of Aragon and Castile. However, as is the way with most expansionist powers, the Navarrese area of control ultimately fragmented, breaking into a number of separate feudal kingdoms. Pamplona, the main Basque kingdom, was absorbed into Aragon. The Basque people themselves were concentrated into an area to the north of the central and western Pyrenees.

Down but not out, Navarre make a comeback, but the comeback was short-lived. Navarre was restored in 1157, but in 1199, while Navarre's king was away on a diplomatic mission, Castile, the precursor to modern Spain, invaded and annexed the western Basque Country, leaving what was left of Navarre landlocked. King Alfonso VIII of Castile promised to hand Guipúzcoa and Álava back to Navarre, but promises are meant to be broken. The Castilian king did, however, ratify Navarrese rights in an attempt to gain loyalty. The Navarrese managed to retain a large degree of self-government and privileges which all Castilian (and later, Spanish) monarchs would swear to uphold on oath until the 19th century. These privileges, called *fueros*, provided a guarantee of allegiance to the Spanish kings from their Basque subjects and in turn they had a major impact on the evolution of the Basque Country, preserving as they did a degree of independence and autonomy throughout the years.

From the Middle Ages onwards, the Basques developed a reputation as formidable seafarers and fishermen, they developed the rudder and built boats which took them across the Atlantic in search of whales and cod. Heading ever westward, it's believed that Basques may have discovered North America hundreds of years before Columbus – it's a documented fact that Basque sailors made up the bulk of

Columbus's crew.

Back on dry land, the Basque Country in the Late Middle Ages was ravaged by local power struggles. The War of the Bands saw families fighting each other to gain control in Navarre and Biscay. As the Middle Ages drew to a close, the Basques found themselves fighting for survival, sandwiched as they were between the two rising superpowers of France and Spain. Most Basques ended up in Spain, where their independence was protected by the *fueros*. In France, Basque regional laws suffered a gradual erosion of status. Lower Navarre was fully absorbed at a fairly early stage and by the 17th century, the last component of the northern Basque Country was permanently attached to France. The French Revolution of 1789 marked the end of Basque privileges, in favour of a centralised and unified French state.

Meanwhile, back in Spain, the southern Basque Country was embroiled in disputes with the Spanish authorities. Rights guaranteed by the *fueros* began to be ignored as centralised government started to assert itself. Matters were made worse during the Peninsular War. Biscay and Navarre were granted civil constitutions by the French army of occupation, but then the Spanish Constitution of Cadiz talked of one sole Spanish nation and the civil constitutions were overturned.

With the threat of an end to any form of self-rule or self-determination hanging over their heads, the Basque provinces turned away from the new liberal Spanish Cortez and backed traditionalist leaders who they believed would defend the ancient order and honour the *fueros*. The Basque provinces, but not all the towns and cities within them, backed Carlos V – it was the beginning of the Carlist Wars.

The First Carlist War went badly for the Basque Country. Forced to surrender, the Basques who had supported Carlos V did so on the basis that their rights would be respected. In 1839, however, the Basques lost their entitlement to create their own laws and enforce them through their own courts, and things were about to get even worse. Ongoing differences led to the Second Carlist War – if the first war had gone badly, the second was a disaster for the Basque Country. Defeat heralded the Law of Abolition of Statutes, which removed all remaining vestiges of Basque autonomy.

Disillusioned by defeat and angry about the lack of autonomy, Sabino Arana established the Basque National Party (PNV) to fight for the right to self-government. A traditionalist, but strategically a forward thinker, Arana encouraged Basque unity by inventing modern nationalistic symbols. Arana gave the Basque Country a flag (based on the Union Jack), a national anthem and a name: Euzkadi.

Ruled by Spanish monarchs and controlled by the Spanish police, many Basques felt that their country was occupied by a foreign power. Simmering discontent was also linked to industrialisation, which brought wealth to some, but created an impoverished urban proletariat, who became increasing receptive to socialist and anarchist ideologies.

Remaining neutral throughout World War I, Spain profited as a result of increased trade. The end of the war, however, brought recession and decline to the Basque industrial heartlands. People wanted change. Encouraged by growing support, the PNV continued to pursue independence. In 1931, at the onset of the Second Spanish Republic, an attempt was made to draw up a single statute for the Basque territories in Spain, but Navarre pulled out of proceedings and the attempt failed.

In 1936, the Spanish Civil War broke out and the Basques were forced to pick sides. Navarre, deeply traditionalist, Catholic and 'Carlist', sided with the Nationalists. The other Basque regions, after a period of doubt and hesitation, supported the Republic, which granted them their coveted autonomous Basque state. Sadly, for the Basques, autonomy was short-lived: it died along with the Republic, defeated by Franco's forces.

After the Civil War, Franco instigated a long and vicious campaign of persecution against the Basques, whom he viewed as traitors. Franco believed in one unified Spain, and opposed any kind of regional diversification. The Basque language and the Basque flag were banned. Measures were put in place to remove all Basque cultural events and Basque parents were refused the right to give their children Basque names. Hundreds of Basques emigrated to the French Basque Country or into exile abroad.

Franco kept Spain out of World War II, but the Basques hoped that after defeating Hitler and Mussolini, the Allies would focus their forces on fascist Spain. The Allies, however, were tired of war and short of cash, consequently Franco remained unchallenged and firmly in power. Initially, the Basques could at least count on the sympathy of the Western powers, but that changed when the spread of communism and the rise of the Soviet Union became the greater fear. To the utter horror of the Basques, Franco was recast by the West as the protector of Western values against the red menace.

In the 1950s, pro-independence Basque students sought to counter Franco's power by forming Euskadi ta Askatasuna (Basque Fatherland and Liberty), or ETA. The principal aim of ETA was to establish an independent socialist Basque state, straddling northern Spain and the southern end of the French Atlantic coast.

Making its first appearance in 1959, ETA was primarily a splinter group born from a schism within the PNV. The movement quickly radicalised and called for violent insurrection against Franco's regime. Attacks were launched against the Guardia Civil, the Spanish paramilitary police and Franco's hierarchy. In 1973, ETA struck a blow that would change the course of Spanish history: they assassinated Luis Carrero Blanco, Franco's right-hand man and chosen successor. The attack marked the beginning of the end for Franco's regime. Franco managed to remain in power for nearly forty years, but after his death in 1975, the leadership of the country was handed to King Juan Carlos, who re-established democracy.

The return of democracy marked a return to more tolerant times. Regional languages such as Basque no longer had to be spoken in secret: they took on greater value and became promoted national languages within Spain. As well as being free to speak their native tongue, some aspects of power were given back to the regions, and in 1979 the Basque provinces of Guipúzcoa, Biscay and Álava were granted autonomy, within the parameters set by the Constitution. The province of Navarre, however, refused to join Euskadi and negotiated a separate status.

With Basque autonomy finally established, rifts began to appear within the Nationalist movement. Some celebrated the new status given to Basque provinces, while others wanted to continue their struggle for total and complete independence. It was within this context that some ETA members continued their terrorist activities, despite the return of democracy. Their political branch, the Batasuna party founded in 1978, relayed their message to the public and held seats in parliament.

Political violence worsened in the 1980s, escalated by the creation of the Antiterrorist Liberation Group (GAL), a paramilitary wing of the Spanish police that hunted down and murdered ETA members across the border in French territory. Such clandestine activities led to political scandal in Spain. The French, naturally upset about what was happening on their own soil, reacted by allowing ETA suspects to be extradited back into Spain; ETA reacted by stepping up their attacks and acts of violence. In 1984, the Basque Country was on high alert.

Back at Ariana's uncle's house, the party continued. Spirits replaced wine and conversations became increasingly unguarded – it was obvious where the family's sympathies lay. This was a proud family with a proud heritage. Some things can be forgiven and forgotten, but not everything. Some things are worth fighting for, but you've got to know when to stop.

Knowing my own limits, I knew when to stop. Unfortunately, I had passed that particular point several drinks earlier. The bathroom was occupied, so I ventured back out into the garden. Fresh air revived my spirit, but too much spirit was unfortunately the problem. I lay down, I looked at the moon, the stars and the remaining rabbits – I apologised to any that cared to listen.

We stayed at Ariana's uncle's house for a couple of days. Ariana's gran continued on her road to recovery and Ariana's family couldn't have been warmer or more welcoming. I remember one particularly hot afternoon, sitting down to eat a full traditional English roast dinner: Ariana's family had wanted to make me feel like I was at home. Once we were sure that Ariana's gran would be okay, we decided to move on, but we wouldn't be heading home. We both wanted to spend some more time exploring San Sebastian. We booked a room in small cheap *hostal,* situated at the far end of La Concha.

I think it would be difficult not to fall in love with San Sebastian. The situation of the town is simply stunning. Our *hostal* was located on the western edge of La Concha, which must be one of the most beautiful urban beaches in Europe. The old town and the port are located at the eastern end of the beach. The beach lies in a classic arcuate bay, framed and partially enclosed by two curved headlands, which are separated by two narrow stretches of open water on either side of the Isla Santa Clara. The island lies smack bang in the centre of the concordant bay. The bay itself is surrounded by low hills, which serve to accentuate the overall beauty of the area. Geology has been kind to San Sebastian, but so has design. The beach is backed by a wonderful promenade, complete with pretty gardens, intricate railings and ornate street lamps. Backlit at night, the illuminations reflected by the cool Atlantic, emphasised the golden sand of the bay and gave structure to a view that simply took our breath away.

The old town itself is another example of classic design which proves that occasionally man can compete with nature. I'm not suggesting that the destruction of the original town by British troops in 1813 would have been a good time for the resident population, but the phoenix that rose from the ashes still impresses. The original town, which was completely burnt to the ground, was rebuilt in neoclassical style. The area was simply beautifully: the austere, systematic architecture provided a wonderful backdrop and home to narrow streets and lively bars. The town looked both impressive and sophisticated and it exuded a cultured air. Home to an international film festival and an annual jazz festival, San Sebastian is also renowned for its dining clubs and gastronomy.

As if by accident, we had discovered our own Eden: a beautiful beach, a stunning location, a rich history and an atmospheric old town full of delight. Surrounded by temptation, we spent our days on the beach and our nights wandering the old town in search of food, drink and entertainment.

San Sebastian had become our garden of delight, but apples certainly weren't the most tempting thing on the menu. The bars in San Sebastian appeared to be competing with each other in their attempts to produce the most elegant, the most elaborate and the most sensational tasting food that they could. Always beautifully arranged, if the look of the *pintxos* wasn't enough to tempt you by themselves, the barmen tried to seal the deal with tantalising descriptions that set us salivating. The snacks, the Basque equivalent of *pinchos*, were usually pierced with cocktail sticks. *Pintxo* is a Basque take on the Spanish word *pincho*, which itself comes from the verb *pinchar*, which means to pierce. Each night we would fill up on cheap hearty food, before heading out on a culinary quest to discover new taste sensations. Unfortunately, our quests were usually curbed by our increasingly desperate financial situation. Like children in a sweet shop, we looked with desire, but gratification was limited by a lack of pesetas.

Sharing one particularly tasty *pintxo* in a particularly lovely bar, I heard shouting and chanting, which unusually rose above the normal sound of the crowd. A barman, alerted to the commotion, walked towards the entrance of his establishment. He looked to his right and then his left, and then promptly told everyone to leave the premises. A customer standing close to the door stuck his head out into the street; he looked right and then left, and then promptly jumped back into the bar as a broken brick whistled past his head. Perhaps unwisely, I poked my head out of the door. The street immediately in front of the bar was empty, apart from a broken brick, but to my left were heavily armed police and to my right was an angry mob armed with sticks, bricks and bottles. Without too much difficulty I predicted a riot, but I couldn't have predicted my next move. I was forcibly pulled back inside the bar by the barman, who then proceeded to pull down a heavy metal security shutter. We were locked in for the night.

It was late, but the bar was still full of customers. Friends and strangers, united by circumstance, quickly became confidants as everyone discussed the situation and the likely outcome of events. It transpired that this particular night was the anniversary of the death of a leading light in the ranks of ETA. The rank and file of ETA had taken to the streets in memory and in protest: conflict, it was suggested, was almost inevitable. Whilst discussions raged inside and violence raged outside, the barmen served a round of free wine and beer. Things were looking up. Shortly afterwards, a barman asked if anyone was hungry and indicated that we could help ourselves to the day's remaining *pintxos*. I didn't need to be asked twice. I had never tasted such fantastic food. Politics, protestors and the police may well have been colliding, but I was enjoying the moment. We were safe, secure and we were very well fed.

A strange kind of party atmosphere lasted into the early hours of the next morning. Political reality had thrown us all together, but once the initial shock died down, people talked and chatted with an air of almost complete indifference. After leaving a suitable gap between the last audible evidence of disturbance and the reopening of the metal shutters, one of the barmen finally suggested that it was safe to leave. We thanked the staff profusely before walking out into the early morning. Detritus littered the street. Bricks, bottles and broken barstools provided evidence of the night before. The evidence of passion, politics, pain and patriotism was all too clear.

THIS IS NOW

Today, the Basque Country enjoys more autonomy than any other region in Spain – it has its own parliament and police force, it controls education and collects its own taxes, but some ETA hard-line supporters remain determined to push for full independence.

Estimates suggest that over the last forty years, ETA has been responsible for over 820 deaths. ETA's victims have included members of the Guardia Civil, Spain's national police force, as well as both local and national politicians who have opposed ETA's separatist demands. Some of these politicians have been native Basques. Innocent bystanders have also been victims and at one time it was announced that all tourists visiting Spain were legitimate targets.

ETA was particularly active in the late 1970s and the early 1980s, when in one year, its violent campaign led to over 100 deaths. Nowhere was safe as violent episodes occurred throughout Spain and the Basque Country. Drive-by shootings took place in San Sebastian and in 1985, two off-duty policemen were shot dead close to the centre of the town.

In more recent times, ETA's activities appear to have declined. ETA has been losing support from amongst its own people and it has come under increasing pressure from coordinated police and political counterterrorism campaigns. Its leadership and its funding have both been successfully targeted.

The assassination of a popular local politician in 1997 marked a major turning point in ETA's popularity and fortunes. Miguel Angel Blanco was kidnapped from his home in front of his wife and children. When the Spanish authorities refused to meet ETA's demands (the release of hundreds of ETA prisoners) he was executed. Public opinion dramatically turned against ETA. Millions took to the streets and demanded an end to violence. The following year ETA announced a ceasefire, but when the Spanish government refused to discuss ETA's demands for independence until the group fully denounced violence, ETA returned to their old ways.

In 2004, bomb attacks in Madrid marked another major turning point. The bombings, which led to 192 deaths and thousands of injuries, were originally falsely blamed on ETA, in what was seen as a political move to garner support for the government in its aim to win an upcoming election. When it became apparent that the bombings were the work of an extremist Islamic group, the electorate rejected the incumbent government and voted in the Socialist Party. The bombings did, however, have the effect of uniting the whole country against violence and terrorism. At the time it was thought that ETA no longer believed that they could achieve their aims by violent means, but after a hiatus, their attacks unfortunately continued.

Recent years have seen a never-ending round of ceasefires, broken promises, violent outbursts, arrests and more ceasefires. Presently we are in a period of relative peace, but whilst ETA has pledged to refrain from violent separatist struggle, the separatist movement itself has not been denounced and ETA have been slow to give up their arms. In actual fact, ETA's announcement, which pledged an end to violence, reinforced their struggle for the Basque homeland at the same time, but admittedly through the use of democratic means.

Democracy has to be the way forward. Events in other regions of Spain (Catalonia and Galicia), and in other countries (the Scottish referendum) show that regionalism is still very much an item on the political agenda. In an uncertain world, what is certain is that the question of Basque independence won't go away.

STARING AT THE SEA

That Was Then

Dawn broke through the darkness as the sun rose between Isla Santa Clara and the old port. To the west the skies were still an inky-black, but to the east a white disc appeared. Surrounded by a golden halo, it cast an iridescent glow. Light triumphed as the night sky became increasingly and inexorably infused with colour; shades ranged from hazy oranges to deep purples – Isla Santa Clara and the old port were silhouetted by contrast. The sea gently rippled and a beam of white light lengthened and broadened as it stretched out towards the shore. The light highlighted both the texture of the sea and the texture of the sand. Gazing skyward once again, colours merged and morphed, before brightness began to bring everything into clearer focus.

Ever since I'd arrived in Malaga, I'd loved everything about Spain. I'd been excited about visiting, but everything had exceeded expectations. I'd loved the culture, the climate and the people, but as I stood and watched the sunrise over San Sebastian, my love of all things Spanish was confirmed beyond doubt,

reasonable or otherwise – it wasn't exactly a life-changing moment, but it was an epiphany of sorts.

THIS IS NOW

I looked at the buffet breakfast and promised myself that I wouldn't overeat – some promises are meant to be broken. The food looked incredible: a range of tasty dishes stretched out before us – all elegantly and irresistibly presented. A Parador breakfast is a joy to behold.

I'm a firm believer in the theory that breakfast is the most important meal of the day. I also believe that a leisurely breakfast, prepared by someone else, is one of the nicest meals of the day – well, one of the three nicest. I don't understand why anyone wouldn't want to eat breakfast. We all 'fast' while we are asleep; who wouldn't want to break that 'fast' in the morning? It makes no sense.

We found an outside table which offered fantastic views to the Mediterranean coastline, similar to those afforded by the Balcon de Europa; then, after being served tea and coffee, we went back inside the hotel to make the first of our many selections. The choice was bewildering. Fruit juices, cava, cereals, fresh fruit, yoghurt, pastries and cakes (of various types), cold meats, Iberico ham, chorizo, cheeses, tortillas, bacon, eggs, *migas*, toast, preserves and a whole variety of different types of bread. I didn't know where to start, so I randomly chose a dish and decided to work my way around the table. I didn't know when to stop; I lost count of the times I revisited the table, but at least movement aided digestion. If gluttony is a sin, we were all guilty, but we knew that we probably wouldn't have to eat again for the rest of the day.

With breakfast over and the rest of the day stretching ahead of us, we dragged ourselves away from the seemingly self-replenishing buffet and made one last trip to the beach via the glass elevator. After taking a pleasant stroll along the foreshore, which involved nothing more taxing than watching the start of a triathlon, we returned to the hotel and packed our processions into the car. We said a quiet thank you to David (wherever he might have been) and headed towards Chite.

Despite our previous night's change of heart, we weren't particularly sad to be leaving Nerja. The Parador, the Balcon de Europa and the old town had been fantastic, but we thought that in one night we had exhausted most of what the town had to offer. It wasn't really our kind of place. Chite sounded much more like our cup of tea. I knew a little bit about the village from conversations with Grahame. I knew, for instance, that the village was situated midway between Granada and the Costa Tropical, and that it was located in the Lecrin Valley, on the edge of the Alpujarra; a natural and historic region on the southern slopes of the Sierra Nevada. I'd seen pictures and I remembered that Chite looked like a traditional Pueblo Blanco: rural, rustic and agricultural. Despite a few ex-pats taking up residence, I was reliably informed that tourism was yet to take hold. It sounded perfect and when we arrived we weren't disappointed. Chite was beautiful, charming and unspoilt. The village was divided into upper and lower sections, both were surrounded by orange groves, almond trees, olive trees, prickly pears and lemon trees. Grahame's friend Stuart's house was in upper Chite.

When I'd booked our accommodation, the only thing I was worried about was the price, which seemed too good to be true. The accommodation, however, was fantastic. Our apartment included three bedrooms: all were en-suite and Tom's even had its own lounge and kitchenette. The two main bedrooms were separated by a deep and quite delightfully refreshing internal plunge pool. The apartment also had a separate kitchen and lounge with a balcony. If that wasn't enough, the building was topped off with a simply massive roof terrace, complete with a gazebo and sunloungers, which offered mountain views in every conceivable direction.

If the accommodation was lovely, so were our hosts. Stuart and his wife Olwyn couldn't have been friendlier or more welcoming. Both from Yorkshire, they were gentle, kind and unassuming, with a keen sense of the absurd and a dry sense of humour. Initially visiting Spain for a holiday, Stuart and Olwyn fell in love with the area and relocated. They bought an old ruin of a town house and converted it themselves. The conversion, which included our apartment, had created a spacious, cool and well-equipped modern house in a traditional style. The building paid testament to Stuart's vision and architectural skills and Olwyn's patience. We liked them both. I think it would be fair to say that we had fallen firmly on our feet.

We unpacked, rested up for a while, explored the centre of the village and then made the most of the facilities offered by our new accommodation: we plunged and we sunbathed. In the evening, despite the fact that we had enjoyed a massive breakfast, we walked to another village, Talara, in search of food and drink. Chite is lovely, but it doesn't have any shops or restaurants and it only has one bar, which hardly ever seemed to be open. Talara was a less pretty, but more functional village. There were several restaurants and bars to choose from. We chose Bar Garvi.

I was particularly looking forward to our drinks and food, because I had been told that in the province of Granada, wherever and whenever you order a drink, you receive free tapas. Back in the 1980s, I remember receiving complimentary olives and sunflower seeds in some bars, but I don't remember being offered anything more elaborate or substantial and I don't remember it being a city-wide, let alone a province-wide, phenomenon. The concept sounded like another deal that was too good to be true, but not for the first time, we were more than pleasantly surprised. The old adage that there is no such thing as a free lunch doesn't apply here. We ordered our drinks, which cost about 2 euros each, and then shortly afterwards a plate containing four portions of deliciously tasty and wholesome food arrived. Our appetites returned. After ordering a few more drinks, we were delighted to receive yet another plate of even more delicious food. We didn't always know what we were eating, but the whole 'Russian roulette' approach to food has always thrilled and excited me – it's good to try different dishes and eat food which is out of your normal comfort zone. Thinking that it was too early to stop, we ordered one final round of drinks and the accompanying free tapas reached even higher standards – what a fantastic way to eat.

We discovered that bars in Granada reward loyalty – the quality of the tapas usually improves with each additional round of drinks. Bar Garvi had been a fantastic place to be introduced to the concept of free tapas. The food was great and the service was fast and friendly. The bar and all the other bars in Talara, were packed, and it wasn't difficult to understand why – it would be nigh on impossible to eat and drink at home for less than it cost to eat out. Two or three portions of free tapas, depending on the bar in question, are about the calorific equivalent of a normal meal. I remember thinking that it must be difficult for bars to give away free tapas and stay in business, but alcohol is cheap in Spain, and wholesome free tapas, whilst delicious, are usually made from cheap ingredients. The fact that all the bars are often full must also help. Another fact that I discovered later about free tapas in Granada is that there are 'student' bars, where the free tapas are wholesome and tasty, and 'gourmet' bars, where the portions are small, but high-end and deliciously refined. I was looking forward to investigating both types.

By now it was late and it had been a long day, so even though more and more people kept arriving at the bar, we headed back to Chite. As we walked, the moon and the stars shone and lights flickered in the Lecrin Valley. We were a little tired, but we were happy and content. We looked at the distant silhouettes of mountains and picked lemons from some of the trees that we passed en route. We said a quick '*buenas noches*' to other late-night walkers and to villagers who sat outside their doorways enjoying the cool of night. We walked past an orange grove and smelt some fragrant local flowers. We thought about our day and marvelled at our good fortune – we were just about as satisfied as life allows. We headed to our beds and slept soundly until rudely awakened the next morning.

Chite, may not have had any shops, but it wasn't short of places where you could buy things! Confused? So were we on our first morning, when we woke to the collective sound of numerous car horns, which seemed to be honked with quite alarming frequency. We discovered later that our dawn chorus was provided by a number of different mobile shopkeepers, who called and sold their wares from the backs of their cars and vans. The village was actually quite well served; you could buy vegetables, meats, fish and bread. Once we got used to the idea and worked out exactly when and where the different mobile services stopped, we enjoyed freshly baked bread and croissants nearly every morning.

As we were up bright and early (slightly earlier than intended), we decided that on our first full day in Chite we would drive out and explore Lanjaron, a local spa town famous for its mineral water, which is sold throughout Spain. Lanjaron, is also home to a small but quite magnificent Moorish castle. Taking our life in our hands, we headed up through the mountains; some of the roads were a little scarier to drive on than I had imagined – it wasn't just the heat that was making me sweat. Lanjaron is an ancient town, which has Roman origins, but when we arrived it was obvious that little from that period still remains. Today, architecturally at least, the town more closely resembles an Austrian alpine village, rather than a Roman or even a traditional Spanish one; perhaps the 'Austrian' look was thought a fitting design for a spa town. Lying beneath the town, perched on a large, rocky outcrop, is the castle. The castle provides evidence of Lanjaron's former importance and status as the medieval gateway to the Alpujarra. It was here, in 1500, that the Moorish population in Spain made one of its last great stands. Forced to retreat into this seemingly impenetrable fortress, the Moors were defeated by weight of numbers and artillery. Sadly, hundreds died, and their leader, the so-called 'Black Captain', allegedly threw himself to his death from the parapets rather than face the indignity of capture. The Christian forces had had to battle their way towards the castle, but we approached by way of a beautiful and peaceful park (El Parque del Salado). Initially following a stream, we descended steeply through eucalyptus trees and exotic plants, before climbing even more steeply to reach our destination. The ancient walls of the castle were supported by structured beams; some parts looked a little rickety, but a series of metal walkways allowed access to most areas. The castle was an impressive and an evocative place to be – the views were amazing. After we had explored all nooks and crannies, we walked back through the town and thought to ourselves that it would be good to return and visit in June. Every year, on 23 June, a water festival takes place. The San Juan Fiesta de Agua y Jamón incorporates a massive water fight, which involves everyone who lives in the area, including the local fire brigade.

After returning to Chite for a late afternoon nap, we headed out once again. We had really enjoyed our tapas at Bar Garvi, but we'd been told that the best free tapas served in the local area could be found at El Rincon de Miguel, in Niguelas. The village of Niguelas, only a few kilometres away from Chite, turned out to be a charming place with a very dramatic location. Situated next to the steep slopes of the 3,000-metre-high Pico del Caballo, Niguelas is the highest municipality in the Lecrin Valley. We took a wander around the village and we were rewarded with a number of fantastic panoramic views. The village itself had a rustic, rundown sort of charm. Some buildings had obviously been recently renovated, but Niguelas had an authentic and honest character about it.

Our bar of choice, El Rincon de Miguel, was located on the outskirts of the village. At first, we walked past the bar; it was an easy mistake to make. The building that houses the bar is quite small and apart from a few folded-down chairs and tables, which could have belonged to an adjacent residential property, there were few visible signs to suggest whether or not the bar actually existed. When we realised that El Rincon de Miguel did exist, there were few signs to indicate whether it was actually open or not. Slightly worryingly, there weren't any customers apart from ourselves. It's fair to say that nothing about the exterior of the building gave us much faith in El Rincon de Miguel's hallowed culinary reputation.

More in hope than expectation, Tania and I headed inside, while the boys set up a table outside. Like most small Spanish bars, the interior was dimly lit. One of the few sources of light came from a TV, which blared out at full volume. As our eyes adjusted to the lack of light, we felt our way towards the counter. The limited amount of available floor space had been further diminished by random boxes and crates which threatened to trip us up at any moment. The kitchen, which was partially visible, appeared to be on a similar scale to the bar. It was hard to see how anyone could cook for themselves in such a small space, let alone cook for other people. We talked about leaving and finding somewhere else, but the barman caught our eye. We had reached the point of no return.

Walking back outside to join the boys, we were pleased to discover that some other customers had arrived – at least we were no longer alone. I looked at my watch: perhaps we had been too eager to eat – I should have remembered that the Spanish don't like to eat too early. Shortly afterwards, a waiter brought drinks over to our table as yet more customers arrived. It didn't take long for nearly all the tables and chairs to fill up – perhaps we had made a wise decision after all. Then, just as if to confirm my thoughts, a piping-hot spinach and tuna tortilla was brought over to our table, accompanied by some crunchy rustic bread. The tortilla was exquisite, it had been cooked to perfection: runny in the middle, it melted in the mouth. We savoured the flavours and we used our bread to wipe the plates clean. It was soon time for some more food, so we ordered another round of drinks. Our second plate of tapas arrived in moments rather than minutes. We were presented with garlic, cheese and ham filled bagels. Each morsel of the food was delicious. After devouring the flavoursome snacks, we concurred that once again the quality of the food was increasing with each successive order. We were now fairly full, but the food had been exceptional, so we ordered yet another round of drinks. Just when we thought the quality of the food couldn't get any better, four portions of bread arrived, each topped off with garlic-infused pork, Iberico ham and a quail's egg – it was simply divine. One can only imagine the quality and the standard of food that would have come next if we had continued to order. We realised that we should have had more faith in Grahame's recommendation and in Jose's Law. We made a mental note to return and visit El Rincon del Miguel again, then we headed for home.

Although we were more than content to be staying in Chite, Tania and I did feel a little guilty about the fact that the boys had been deprived of a beach holiday. With this thought in mind, we headed to Salobrena. We were a little concerned that guidebooks described Salobrena in a similar way to Nerja, but when we arrived it was evident that they were very different places. The Old Town of Salobrena sits on top of a rocky outlier – it was both attractive and impressive. Traditional (and by now familiar) whitewashed houses clung tightly to the steep slopes of the outlier, which was topped off by a majestic 10th-century Moorish castle. Newer developments linked the Old Town to the beach, but whilst some of the buildings looked out of place, most had been sympathetically styled. Both old and new sections of the town were almost completely surrounded by sugarcane plantations. Salobrena has certainly been developed with tourism in mind, but it was far smaller and far less developed than Nerja.

The beach itself couldn't be described as an undiscovered wilderness, but it had a utilitarian charm about it. Bars and fish restaurants lined the backshore, whilst lines of sunloungers separated the top and bottom of the clean and not overly crowded foreshore. The beach was just fine, but the view from the beach was simply stunning. Limited expectation was followed by amazing revelation. The sea glistened and sparkled – it was inviting and crystal clear. Waves broke gently on the shore, mixing pebbles and fine sediment whilst emitting a calming and soothing clatter. The swash and the backwash were colourless and clear – individual pieces of sand and fragments of shell were clearly visible. Beyond the breaking waves the sea was a translucent green – tiny fish darted one way and then another. Out beyond the sea of green was a sea of blue – a beautiful picture-postcard blue: no need for filters or technological enhancement. The sky mirrored the marine perfection. Without a cloud to be seen, a solid block of azure blue gradually faded out to a clear, calm distant horizon. Throwing financial caution to the wind, we hired two sunloungers and set up camp. The boys wondered why we hadn't hired four sunloungers, but we explained that age has its compensations.

We spent most of our time swimming, reading, sunbathing, chatting and enjoying the view, but we interrupted our standard beach routine to enjoy a fine lunch at one of the beach-based restaurants. A thirty-second stroll transported us from a peaceful paradise to a culinary one. The beach bar-cum-restaurant was by necessity fairly basic, but the fish was fantastic. Sitting on an outside table and staring at the sea whilst crunching sand beneath our toes, we enjoyed two plates of seafood: one fried and one grilled – both were delicious. The food was heart-warmingly full-flavoured, inviting, tempting and sometimes mysterious – it was Spain on a plate. We recognised some of the many different types of fish by taste and sight, but others defied definition and sometimes description – all, however, were divine. The food appeared to be going down well with all the customers in the restaurant, the clear majority of whom appeared to be Spanish; their lively conversations and obvious appreciation of the food, the drink and the moment, reminded me (not for the first time) of just why I love and appreciate Spanish attitudes towards life in general and family in particular. It was good to see large multigenerational groups of people, wining and dining contentedly. The adults drank, laughed and conversed, whilst the children talked and played: they were included and indulged, but not overindulged. Perhaps it's the culture. Perhaps it's the weather. Perhaps it's the food. Who really knows? What's certain, however, is the fact that the Spanish appear to have got things just right.

Feeling full and more than a little satisfied, Tania and I went for an after-dinner stroll along the foreshore. The beach was beginning to fill up with sun worshippers, so we walked along the line of the breaking waves. There was still space on the beach, but the distance between beach towels and sunloungers was noticeably diminishing. The clear majority of the new and old arrivals were Spanish, but a few scarlet and a few pale-faced tourists were clearly evident; their complexions gave away their north European heritage. I like to think that after a few weeks in Spain, I could be mistaken for a local; I like to think that after a few weeks in the sun I blend into the crowd – but the truth of the matter is somewhat different. I might think that I look tanned and 'golden brown', but I'm usually a bright shade of red. I might think that I look Spanish, but my Englishness is usually all too evident.

We headed towards El Peñon, a rocky outcrop which divides the beach into two. Leaving other beachgoers behind us, we enjoyed some moments of isolation, peace and quiet. We walked and scrambled over the rocky outcrop, heading back towards the sea; we were rewarded with yet more stunning views, but also with one less than splendid one. Once again, I stood and stared. To the east and the south all was beauty, but to the west Spain revealed its uglier side – Almunecar stood out like a sore thumb. Towering apartment blocks and hotels broke the skyline, destroying what must once have been a wonderful scene. Little or no effort had been made to blend the modern monuments to commercialism and mass tourism with the traditional architecture or the natural configuration of the landscape. It was enough to make you weep.

Looking at the view, I thought about Laurie Lee, author of *Cider with Rosie* and many other glorious books. I wondered what he would have thought about recent developments. Born and brought up in the Cotswolds, Laurie Lee left the security of family, cider and Rosie, and travelled to Spain in 1934. His journey through Spain is described in his autobiographical book *As I Walked Out One Midsummer Morning*. Lee's decision to travel to the country was based upon nothing more than a sense of adventure and the fact that he knew one phrase of Spanish, '*Puede por favor dame un vaso de agua?*' – 'Will you please give me a glass of water'. Over the course of a year, Lee walks through Spain, armed with nothing more than a violin and a lust for life. Travelling from Galicia to Andalusia, he poetically and prosaically describes a country caught in a moment of time. He encounters extreme poverty, desolation and extreme beauty. His youthful innocence and wondrous nature capture Spain on the edge of an abyss. Lee has little money, so he survives by busking and relying on the generosity of others. He sleeps at night, either wrapped in a blanket under the stars or in cheap, rough *posadas*, though occasionally he rests in houses, rewarded by the warm and generous hospitality of poor villagers whom he meets along the way. *As I Walked Out One Midsummer Morning* is a wonderfully evocative account of life in Spain during the bleak years leading up to the Spanish Civil War. After visiting Vigo, Valladolid, Madrid, Seville, Cordoba and Cadiz, Lee finds himself in Almunecar in early 1936. Working in a hotel, Lee describes discussions about rights and revolution. He meets Manolo, the leader of a group of fishermen and labourers, and becomes involved in local politics. In February, the Socialists win the election and a Popular Front begins. In spring, the villagers, in an act of revolt, burn down the local church, but then regret their actions. In the middle of May, there is a strike and the peasants come in from the countryside to lend their support as the village splits between 'Fascists' and 'Communists'. In the middle of July, war breaks out and Manolo helps organise a militia. Granada is held by the rebels, as is Almumecar's neighbour, Altofaro. War comes to Almunecar and to Laurie Lee; he agonises about what to do next. Eventually, plagued by guilt for his new-found friends and comrades, Lee is picked up by a British destroyer from Gibraltar and temporarily returns to the UK.

Back in Slad, near Stroud, Laurie Lee wrestled with his conscience before returning to Spain in 1937 to fight for the Republican cause. In an autobiographical sequel to *As I Walked Out One Midsummer Morning*, called *A Moment of War*, Lee dramatically describes his return to Spain.

Lee crosses over the Pyrenees, alone and in the middle of a snowstorm. Partially frozen and fully frustrated, Lee meets up with some Republican sympathisers. However, suspected of being a Nationalist spy, he is arrested, imprisoned and sentenced to death. Reprieved after a chance encounter, Lee goes on to fight for the International Brigades. Based in Figueres, Valencia, Tarazona, Madrid, Teruel and finally Barcelona, Lee's story is one of hardship and ultimately disillusionment. The optimism of his youth is replaced by the pessimism of a mature reality.

Laurie Lee lost his wartime diaries and wrote the last book in his autobiographical sequence some sixty years after the events he describes; some people have cast doubt on the historical accuracy of his memoir, but it's hard to doubt the authenticity of his experience. Both Laurie Lee's books about Spain are excellent, worthy of reading and rereading. I first read *As I Walked Out One Midsummer Morning* in 1984, and I had been rereading the book since arriving in Chite. Sometimes it's true to say that things are never as good as the first time, but familiarity with Lee's text certainly doesn't breed contempt – I'd been enjoying the book as much, if not more than when I had first read it. Back in the day I shared Lee's wanderlust and optimism; I like to believe that I still do. However, now I can compare his experience of place with mine and I can empathise with his internal conflict. If life teaches us anything, it's to stand up for what we believe in, but it's also to hang onto the things that we love. With my head spinning from thoughts of poetry and prose, I turned away from Almunecar, held Tania's hand and headed back to the beach to read some more.

That Was Then

Yet another car sped past us as we stood by the side of the road holding a small cardboard sign emblazoned with one word – Madrid. In an attempt to save money, we had decided to hitchhike back to Granada, by way of a series of long hops. Oh, the optimism of youth. After about half an hour of being ignored, we decided that we needed to adopt a slightly different hitchhiking strategy. I ducked down out of sight and Ariana continued to hitch on her own. Shortly afterwards a car pulled up about 100 metres away from us. Ariana walked towards the car and I followed on behind. The car drove away, but at least we were making progress – we decided to repeat the tactic. Shortly afterwards another car stopped. Once again, Ariana walked towards the car and I slowly followed on behind. The young male driver didn't look best pleased when he saw me, but he offered us a lift anyway. Linguistic demands meant that Ariana jumped into the front seat and I jumped into the back. 'Excellent – things are working out well,' I thought to myself, before thoughts were interrupted by a strange and overpowering smell: an unpleasant aroma appeared to be emanating from the upholstery. I wound down a window as the car pulled away and the driver struck up a conversation with Ariana. What was that smell? I couldn't place it. Ariana and the driver chatted happily for a while, but then I detected a growing look of concern spread across Ariana's face. Consternation had replaced two-way conversation. 'What's he talking about?' I asked. Ariana turned to face me. 'He's apologising for the smell of blood. Apparently, he's a butcher.' My blood ran cold. The car was an ordinary saloon, it was hardly a butcher's van. I looked towards the rear-view mirror and caught a glimpse of the driver and what I thought was a faintly sinister smirk.

CAMINITO

THIS IS NOW

Location, location, location.

Perception of – and pleasure in – place is all about location, and location is all about site and situation. Chite is situated halfway between a mostly beautiful coastline and an entirely wondrous city; it's surrounded by charming natural and built environments. In addition to its situation, its site leaves little to be desired. Chite is built on the side of a hill, with views up to the Sierra Nevada and down to Lake Beznar. Its elegant setting in the Lecrin Valley provides direct access to a relaxed and traditional lifestyle and to a picturesque yet functional landscape. There's much that can be seen, explored and appreciated without the hassle of having to travel too far.

We hadn't had to travel too far to get to Salobrena, but after a day spent indulging several of my passions in a coastal setting (swimming, reading, eating and relaxing), today seemed like a good day to make the most of Chite's setting and indulge another passion. It was time to go walking, and fortunately the whole family were more than happy to accompany me.

Back in the early 1980s, I was no fan of walking or the outdoors. In fact, I was no fan of anything that really involved effort, perspiration or dressing like a geographer. As a young child I had enjoyed walking: my father was a geography lecturer and we spent many family holidays in Cornwall, Devon and various other parts of the UK, looking at ox-bow lakes, raised beaches and other assorted geographical features. When I was nine, we all climbed to the top of Snowdon. I can still remember the excitement and exhilaration I felt at reaching the summit, thinking I was on top of the world, and being delighted when I was told that I was the highest person in England and Wales. I also remember racing up to the top of granite tors, and being amazed by Wistman's Wood on Dartmoor; the dwarf oaks and long, hanging lichens made the whole place look magical, like something straight out of a tale by Tolkein.

This early taste and enjoyment of walking and the great outdoors was, however, fatally diminished by life as a student. I freely admit that I was keener on strutting and posing, rather than striding out and wearing a cagoule. The

joys of a weekend away in mountain hut paled into insignificance compared to a weekend of drinking and general debauchery at the university bar. Friends on my course (Geography) tried to persuade me about the joys of walking, God forbid climbing, and even worse camping, but I choose a path of comfort and indoor pastimes: anyway, it's hard to enjoy the outdoors when you're scared that the rain will flatten your hair.

My reluctance to put one foot in front of the other lasted well into the 1990s, and was only overcome after I was persuaded to spend a long weekend in the English Lake District. Eight hundred and eighty-five square miles of stunning mountains, wondrous valleys and beautiful lakes completely changed my outlook and perspective. Soon I couldn't wait to get out and about, and I embraced walking with all the joy and verve of a religious convert.

I firmly believe that walking is the best way to discover new places and provides real experience of place. It's often the case that we become so obsessed with time and speed, that distance and the experience of place become an inconvenient irrelevance. When I walk, I feel relaxed and I feel content: perhaps it's some primitive desire to be free to roam wherever you want, without any constraints; to be at one with nature, to experience the elements, to feel the wind on your face, to breathe the air and to feel alive. Walking satisfies the soul and medicates the mind.

Today, walking is a big part of my life. My favourite place to walk is still the English Lake District, for me it's one of the best places in the world. I think it's the range of landscapes in a relatively small area, and the fact that you can gaze up at the heights and know that the summits are all achievable. Fortunately, Tania, William and Tom agree – we've spent many family holidays walking and exploring the mountains and valleys of Cumbria. However, although the Lake District is my favourite place to walk, it's certainly not the only place where I like to walk. I was excited about the prospect of walking around Chite, and I was delighted that Stuart, our host, had offered to act as our guide.

Stuart is a keen walker and scrambler. When he lived in the UK, he spent time exploring the English Lake District and the Yorkshire Dales; he also completed several long-distance footpaths. Now, unshackled from the demands of work, he could fully indulge his passion. Once settled in Chite, Stuart began to spend more and more time exploring the local area and the Sierra Nevada. Initially exploring on his own, Stuart soon discovered likeminded souls and established a twice-weekly walking group, composed of ex-pats and locals alike. We had been reliably informed that Stuart's knowledge of local area, the local mountains and their associated walking trails was second to none. Further proof of this point (if proof was required) was provided by the fact that Stuart had written a book about his completion of the 'Sulayr'. The Sulayr, which means the 'mountains of the sun', is the name given to a 300km footpath which encircles the whole of the Sierra Nevada. The route, composed of traditional paths, animal tracks and cattle routes, is divided into nineteen sections. Several of these sections are rarely visited and large areas of the surrounding countryside are rarely explored.

Our planned walk around Chite was less of an adventure and more of an amble, but expectations were high. We met up with Stuart and walked towards the lower section of the village. We headed past the small, but perfectly formed local church and then continued downhill. Narrowing paths and tracks guided us through a veritable garden of delight. Orange groves, lemon trees, olives, figs, pomegranates, blackberry bushes and fantastically shaped giant cacti provided interest, colour and delectation. Much of the planting appeared to be haphazard, but the agricultural landscape was divided into plots. The individual plots were not always easy to distinguish, but all were individually owned and individually watered. A series of earthen, stone and concrete ditches separated and crossed the different parcels of land. Some of the ditches were open and some were covered, but they all provided a regular water supply.

The ditches, or *acequias*, form part of an ancient irrigation system, originally created by the Moors.

The Spanish word *acequia* derives from the Arabic *al saquiya*, which means 'the bearer of water' or 'water conduit'. The name is apt, because *acequias* are gravity fed flumes, which carry water from the high mountains to the local villages and fields. The Moors developed this technology in North Africa, and introduced it into the Iberian Peninsula in the 8th century. The introduction of water management systems transformed many formally barren areas and brought life to the foothills of the Sierra Nevada.

The *acequias* are usually silent and dry, but once or twice a week the parched ditches fill up as torrents of water descend noisily from on high. The water rages and races downhill, but small dams and sluice gates allow individuals to access the life-giving elixir. The importance of the technology to the area cannot be overstated. A measure of the level of this importance can be gauged from the Spanish reaction to the Moriscos rebellion in the Alpujarra. The Moriscos were the nominally Catholic descendants of originally Muslim families. Forced to convert to avoid expulsion after a failed Moorish uprising, the Moriscos rebelled in 1568. Their uprising and eventual defeat led to the expulsion of almost all of the remaining Moriscos from Andalusia. However, almost all is not everyone. Each and every village in the Alpujarra, was allowed to retain two Moriscos families to ensure that the *acequias* continued to function and the water continued to flow.

Following our own course, we walked and talked, and we sampled and tasted the local produce: ripe figs, tasty almonds, blackberries, pomegranates and succulent but sharp oranges. Stuart explained that the small oranges had probably been left over from the previous harvest. 'Nobody would have wanted them' – I could taste why. To be fair to the oranges, they weren't in season, but the lemons were. Oranges ripen from green to orange over winter and are usually harvested in March, but lemons can be harvested all year round. The lemon trees in the Lecrin Valley contained fruit at all stages of ripeness – colours ranged from deep greens to bright yellows. If the *acequias* had been full, water would have been rushing down the hillside and watering the oranges and lemons. Any water remaining after the land had been soaked would have ended up in the local reservoir at the foot of the hill; waste not, want not. As we tracked down the hillside, the reservoir came into clearer focus. We were rewarded with a quite magnificent sight. The turquoise water of Lake Beznar shimmered as it reflected the pure blue of the Andalusian sky.

The walk was a real joy from beginning to end. The area was beautiful and tranquil, our route was picturesque and peaceful. It was fascinating to be guided by a local expert: Stuart shared his knowledge with us and nature surrounded us. We enjoyed each other's company and marvelled at the hidden wonders of the Lecrin Valley. We were definitely off the beaten track. One might have thought that the area would be a magnet for locals and tourists alike, but we didn't pass or see anyone else for the whole time that we were out and about. We did, however, pass a number of isolated *corjitos*.

In the *campo*, or countryside, house-building is restricted, but *corjitos* are permitted. *Corjitos* are small, shepherd's-hut-like constructions. Theoretically, legally and historically, they should only be just about the right size to accommodate one person who might have to sleep overnight whilst tending his or her crops. They are (or should be) extremely basic: any services other than a water supply would be considered unnecessarily luxurious. Nevertheless, we passed several *corjitos* that were far from basic. Many had been unofficially extended to include extra floors, additional rooms, sun terraces and swimming pools. They were illegal by design and illicit by nature. It would be interesting to observe the outcome of a visit by a local planning officer or an inquisitive mayor. The owners of the *cortijos* would have to claim that their pools were ornate drinking troughs and that their extra rooms were barns or stables.

Returning to Stuart and Olwyn's house, we enjoyed a nice cup of tea before returning to our apartment and resting up during the heat of the afternoon: the plunge pool and the sun terrace were well used. We emerged as the cool of evening approached, ready to explore Chite once again. It transpired that this particular evening represented a first for Chite, a new departure. Chite was hosting its first ever night-time market. Stalls selling second-hand furniture, modern knick-knacks, lighting, vintage clothing, illuminated glassware, mounted boars' heads, stuffed ducks, food, drink and what was often just a load of 'old tat' lined the narrow streets. Some of the stallholders were Spanish, but most, along with the clientele, were 'Middle Englanders' who thought that they weren't. Just where all these people had come from was difficult to tell. Perhaps a flight had landed from Totnes or Islington, or perhaps they had emerged from behind twitching shutters in the immediate locale. A faint whiff of dope filled the air and a faint whiff of 'fake' filled the neighbourhood. Some local Spanish people looked on with bemused indifference.

We decided to leave 'Little Britain' and headed towards Grahame's house. Grahame hadn't suddenly returned to Spain, but he'd told us to pop round and visit in his absence. He had forewarned the present occupants about our imminent appearance and they in their turn had confirmed his invitation, but no official time or date had been set. When we arrived, there were few signs of life – shutters were drawn and all was quiet. We knocked anyway, more in hope than expectation. Just as we were about to turn away, silence was broken. A booming voice emerged from behind an exquisitely designed clithridiate doorway, that sat within a much larger rectangular door. 'Come in, come in, don't stand on ceremony.' We followed the clear command, stepped through the 'keyhole' and descended a short flight of steps.

The voice belonged to Richard, who rushed over to greet us. I winced as my hand was painfully compressed. Richard's handshake was as tough and imposing as he was, but Richard was a gentle giant: friendly, welcoming and instantly likeable. We had interrupted Richard whilst he was in the middle of cooking. He informed us that his sister and her family had just arrived from the UK, and they would be arriving here at Grahame's house at any moment. We apologised for visiting at such an inconvenient time and made our excuses to leave. 'Don't be so English,' he said, before pouring us drinks and inviting us to stay and share the food that he was preparing.

Richard was baking pizzas in a purpose-built outdoor oven located in a patio area adjacent to the basement of the house. The patio was planted with vines and wisteria, which would have provided shade during the heat of the day. The patio area incorporated a plunge pool and a fish pond. Beyond the patio a beautifully landscaped garden planted with palms, mature figs and orange trees gave the house a feeling of permanence which argued against its relatively recent construction.

Grahame's house looked traditionally Spanish, but it incorporated many modern design features. The rear of the house was southward facing, but an arched outer wall provided protection from the worst of the summer sun. Small traditional windows on the northern face of the building minimised heat gain and loss, whilst large shaded windows on the southern side provided a sense of light and airiness. The incorporation of high performance insulation helped to maintain a reasonably comfortable and constant temperature.

We discovered that Richard had been living in Spain for fourteen years with his wife, Emma, and their daughters, Lauren and Poppy. He had arrived in Spain with grand objectives, but an ambitious building scheme had been hit by recession. Starting again, almost from scratch, he was living in Grahame's basement flat whilst completing odd jobs and a less grand, but still impressive building project in Niguelas. The only things he missed about the UK were family, friends and fishing.

Above the basement flat, the main house was occupied by a friendly young Spanish couple, who were in the process of having their own house renovated. Guillermo ran an outdoor walking and climbing shop, and Antonia was a pharmacist. Initially out when we had arrived, we met the upstairs occupants at just about the same time as we met Richard's sister and her family; both were invited to join the meal. Family, friends, neighbours, the known and the unknown, the expected and the unexpected – all were treated with warmth and welcome. Richard and his family entertained everyone. Food, drink and conversation flowed as friends and strangers bonded. It was all very Spanish.

The following day saw us return to Salobrena; we enjoyed the experience just as much as we had the first time. During the evening we stayed in and around Chite, and amongst other things we visited the 'bar with no name'. Sometimes open, but more often than not closed, Chite's one bar was a subsidised agricultural labourers' bar. The interior was just about as basic as bars can get. There were a couple of tables, but there were hardly any chairs. A few pictures decorated the mostly bare walls: somewhat bizarrely, a portrait of the Pope was flanked by two pictures of topless glamour models. The range of drinks was limited, but the drinks were cheap. The barman was largely conspicuous by his absence – it was an experience.

Forever willing to seek out new experiences, the following day we headed out for a new kind of walking experience – a river walk. We teamed up with Stuart and headed towards Saleres. Our objective was the Barranco de Luna. Without Stuart's help, the start of the walk would have been nigh on impossible to find. Even with Stuart, it was difficult to locate, and he'd completed the walk several times before. The gorge and river were hidden from the roadside, but after descending into a valley and making a couple of failed attempts to access the river through some quite viscous vegetation, we were eventually able to start. If truth be told, this is a little travelled route and the hidden nature of the river added to our anticipation.

We started the walk as we meant to go on – our feet fully submerged in the cool water of the river. As we headed upstream, along a winding route, the narrow gorge grew in height and stature and the river deepened. Almost imperceptible, not only our feet, but our ankles, knees and finally our thighs were embraced by the current. The water was crystal clear. Pebbles, stones and boulders littered the riverbed, occasionally impeding progress. We passed through rapids and climbed up waterfalls. At some points there were boulders above as well as below us. Huge rocks had been trapped in mid-fall by the twisting and turning narrow top of the gorge. It was difficult to walk under these boulders without at least some sense of trepidation and fear. The boulders looked like they had been stuck since the beginning of time, but all things must fall – we secretly prayed that they wouldn't fall on us.

Almost at the highest point of the gorge, beds of limestone bristled with fossils. In amongst the cliff face, ammonites and belemnites were clearly visible. Past and present merged seamlessly, as shadows and shade interspersed with shafts of sunlight provided moments of colour and contrast. Deep green vegetation, translucent water and shimmering rocks and stones of every imaginable hue transported us to a new reality. The Barranco de Luna was a magical delight.

Unfortunately, all was over too soon. The gorge petered out. We emerged from the river and entered an orange grove. Our route had only been about 3km long, but the walk had been a wonderful experience from beginning to end. The gorge had certainly packed a punch. We thanked Stuart, who responded by suggesting that if we had liked the Barranco de Luna, we'd be sure to love 'El Caminito del Rey'.

That Was Then

The risks associated with hitchhiking are actually far less than many people perceive them to be. I remember reading about a Californian study which concluded that hitchhikers were not disproportionately more likely to be victims of crime. Such information was, however, no more than cold comfort. Fanciful images replayed themselves in my over-imaginative imagination as we headed along the dusty highway.

Sweat-streaked cheeks, a grizzled chin and vacant yet staring eyes were framed in the rear-view mirror. Our driver looked like a serial killer, but then again, what do serial killers look like? I felt both nervous and nauseous. The stench of blood was overwhelming. Ariana looked increasingly concerned, but she gamely kept up a conversation with our travelling *carnicero*. I tried to follow their conversion as I began to contemplate escape routes, but I was somewhat distracted by the not-so-faint aroma of death. Perhaps we should have caught a train or travelled by bus. Hindsight is a wonderful thing. They say that it's better to travel hopefully than to arrive. I hoped that reality would be better than anticipation. Reality used to be a friend of mine.

You should never judge a book by its cover, unless it's written by Jeffrey Archer, or unless by 'book' you mean the driver of a saloon car that smells of blood. Angel, as he was called, did little to dispel our fears. Initially chatty and friendly, he became increasingly less so as the journey continued. Nervous, twitchy and slightly obsessive – he was definitely on the spectrum. He grew visibly agitated when Ariana spoke in English and he spent the majority of the journey staring at her chest rather than at the road ahead. We hatched a plan.

I feigned illness and Ariana indicted that we needed to stop in the next village. A somewhat reluctant Angel parked by the roadside. I rubbed my stomach as Ariana informed Angel that I felt sick (which wasn't far from the truth). Accompanied by Angel, we went to sit down in a local bar. Angel kept looking at his watch and became increasingly agitated. Ariana told Angel that I needed time to recover and that he should carry on without us. Angel took one last look at his watch and Ariana's chest before kissing us both on both cheeks and heading off. He spoke briefly to the barman on his way out, but then he was gone. As Angel's car disappeared into the distance we both breathed a sigh of relief.

We were relieved, but we were going nowhere fast. We needed to find a way to get back to Granada. Consigning hitchhiking to history, Ariana chatted to the barman and discovered that a local bus would be able to take us back to San Sebastian. From San Sebastian we would have to pick up a coach or a train. We would just have to accept that we had made a false start and put this morning's expedition down to experience. However, we were concerned about our experience and discussed whether or not we should pass on our concerns about Angel to the relevant authorities. As we discussed the situation, we ate to satisfy our hunger and drank to settle our nerves. The food was excellent, but it was soon time to go – we had a bus to catch. 'La cuenta por favor,' I asked. 'Es gratis señor . El carnicero ha pagado.' I looked from the barman towards Ariana. 'The butcher has paid our bill,' she translated.

Not only had Angel paid our bill, but he'd asked the barman to make sure that we were okay. Angel was well known to the barman, because he supplied the bar with meat. We mentioned his car and we were told that Angel's usual van was off the road. According to the barman, Angel was a great 'hombre', who regularly and generously gave lifts to friends and travellers, or in our case ungrateful tourists.

Apparently, the only time you can judge a book by its cover is when it's written by Jeffrey Archer. With a sense of guilt and frustration, we trudged to the bus stop and resigned ourselves to the inevitable. Granada was still a long way away, and for a while at least, we would be heading in the wrong direction.

THIS IS NOW

Subsequent research informed us that El Caminito del Rey (the 'little pathway of the king') was a walkway, pinned along the steep, high walls of a narrow gorge in El Chorro, near Alora and Ardales. I say walkway, but there are actually two routes: an original one that has fallen into disrepair and which is now closed to the public, and a new, improved and far safer one. The walkways and the surrounding landscape looked spectacular; we decided to take Stuart's advice and planned an excursion to visit the area

The original walkway was built so that workers could move materials back and forth between the two hydroelectric power plants of Chorro Falls and Gaitanejo Falls; it also allowed access for inspection and maintenance to a water canal that weaved its way through tunnels in the mountains. The suspended walkway was completed in 1905 after four years of construction. Its present name, El Caminito del Rey, derives from its royal patronage. In 1921, King Alfonso XIII crossed the walkway to mark the inauguration of the dam, Conde del Guadalhorce. The king must have had a serious head for heights, because the original path looks to have been very precarious indeed. Constructed from concrete and resting on steel rails supported by stanchions, few parts of the raised path were wider than a metre and some sections were perched on sheer cliffs hundreds of metres above the ground. It hardly seems possible, but today the original path is even more precarious then when it was first built. Deterioration over time has caused many sections of the original path to collapse, leaving yawning gaps bridged by narrow steel beams. Unfortunately, this deterioration hasn't stopped extreme adventure seekers from trying to complete the walk. Several people have died in recent years, despite the fact that the original route was officially closed in 2001.

Fortunately for us, a new walkway was proposed in 2011. The regional government of Andalusia and the local government of Malaga agreed to share the costs of restoration. The project took three years to complete. The new walkway, which opened in 2015, has retained the essence and much of the thrill of the original route, but it has eliminated the risk. Ageing concrete has been replaced by wooden planks and glass panels, whilst a handrail offers support and security. However, those suffering from acrophobia would be well advised to stay away.

We started our walk, not up in the mountains, but down by a lake. We started our walk, not by striding out, but by ambling around looking for somewhere to eat. We started our walk with great expectations: fortunately, the omens were good. We discovered a nice restaurant and sat outside as a bright sun rose slowly in a perfectly clear blue sky. After a tasty breakfast of *tostada con tomate*, we left El Kiosko, and headed through a small tunnel before joining an extremely picturesque path which took us towards El Chorro gorge and El Caminito del Rey. The area is a geomorphologist's paradise. Jurassic limestones and dolomites form rugged and rolling mountains which, when we visited, were reflected in the turquoise water of the Guadalhorce River. Each feature, fracture and fissure was perfectly mirrored. The mountains were flanked and framed by pines, wild olives and oaks. Our route cut through an undergrowth of rosemary, rock roses, dwarf palms and thyme – the colours and fragrances overwhelmed our senses. Closer to the riverbank, rushes, reeds, tamarisk and oleander, as well as poplar, willow and eucalyptus trees, enhanced an already breathtaking scene.

The walk was a delight, and just like most of the best things in life the first part of the walk was free to everyone and anyone who cared to visit, but we soon reached a checkpoint. We, like everyone else, had had to pre-book tickets to be able to access the main gorge walk. The restoration of El Caminito del Rey has been a real success story: tickets need to be booked weeks, if not months in advance. Visits are timed and groups of about forty people are allowed to enter every thirty minutes. As we waited to be supplied with hairnets and hardhats, we received what would turn out to be some excellent advice. A fellow visitor (who had completed the walk several times before) told us to take our time. 'Don't rush,' she said. 'Especially at the start. Savour every moment.'

Following this friendly advice, a series of less friendly but important instructions and warnings were issued in several different languages by the resident staff. Remembering to walk on the right, and not to run or climb, whilst wearing our hairnets and hardhats, we headed through the checkpoint and onto the boardwalk.

The path quickly narrowed and grew increasingly vertical. Gaps between the wooden planks that made up the boardwalk revealed mighty drops into the chasm below. Other members of our group rushed on ahead, but we took our time: chatting, taking photos and gazing in all directions. We looked back towards the hydroelectric plant and the way that we had come, forward towards the narrowing gorge, and down towards the glistening and gurgling river. Time allowed us to become more acclimatised to the height, the narrowness of the path and the sense of exposure. We increasingly forgot our fears. We stopped caressing the solid bulk of the gorge on our right and edged closer to the drop on our left. A mesh of wire and steel was all that separated us from oblivion. Everything about the route exceeded expectation. The whole experience was one to be savoured.

We continued to take our time to take everything in, but eventually the boardwalk turned into a stony track. The stony track headed downhill before sloping gradually upwards once again. It provided less thrills, but no less a thrilling perspective. We walked beside trees and shrubs and enjoyed panoramic mountain views.

The day warmed as the sun rose higher in the sky. We rested at a conveniently located viewpoint, on a conveniently located bench. Sipping some water, I looked towards the mountaintops and spotted several birds of prey taking advantage of the rising thermal columns. Circling majestically, the dark brown raptors were probably looking out for their next meals.

It was a little early for our next meal, but a small snack taken whilst watching the eagles and vultures left us more than a little satisfied. Our enjoyment of the moment was increased by our isolation. We sat alone, unencumbered by the past or the future and untroubled by anyone apart from ourselves. The here and now was everything. Unfortunately, however, we were about to be separated from our sense of separateness. We spent so much time trying to slow down time that the next group of forty visitors caught us up. We waited for the bulk of this group to pass us by before stirring ourselves and heading onwards.

We soon arrived at the second section of boardwalk. Once again, we were surrounded by awe-inspiring scenery, but this time as we gazed down between gaps in the wooden planks we could see not only rocks and water, but also the original walkway. Riddled with holes and with sections where entire chunks had long ago rusted away or fallen into the ravine, the sight was somewhat sobering. It's hard to believe that people ever tried to complete this route. It wasn't hard to believe that some people paid the ultimate price for the experience.

Ahead of us, both the old and the new path looked tiny and precarious: perspective belittled and diminished all apart from the grandeur of the scene. It was at this point of our walk that the impressive gorge looked at its most impressive. The sheer height and scale of the spectacularly steep sidewalls dwarfed everything else. It was a long way down to the river and a dizzyingly long way up to the top of the vertiginous cliffs.

The walk culminated with some glass-floored sections and a hanging bridge. The glass-floored sections in the boardwalk emphasised the drop and the hanging swinging bridge, suspended more than 100m above the ground, emphasised our sense of fear and exposure.

The bridge wasn't a stable structure: it trembled as we trembled – silently shaking with each tremulous footstep. Fortunately, however, it wasn't a bridge too far. Safely back on terra firma, we walked to a bus stop, before being driven back to our original starting point.

Another visit to El Kiosko was followed by a relaxing afternoon spent swimming in and reading beside the Conde de Guadalhorce Reservoir. The stunningly beautiful turquoise-coloured lake, one of three created by the damming of the Guadalhorce and the Guadalteba Rivers, was bordered by pine forest and a number of small beaches. The reservoir was a quiet and tranquil hideaway. We had discovered another piece of paradise. We had discovered Malaga's Lake District.

That Was Then

False starts, slow trains and missed connection meant that our return journey from San Sebastian to Granada took far longer than expected; our expectations for the next day were adjusted accordingly. Rest and relaxation took precedence, but Ariana's flatmate Alison had a different idea about the day ahead. I haven't said much about Alison, and that's because there's not much to say. Alison was quite quiet and usually kept herself to herself, however she was pleasant enough and she liked to walk. She persuaded us to accompany her on a visit to one of Granada's many public parks. Not only were we persuaded to get out and about, but we were also persuaded to take some exercise. I thought that we would be spending our time lying out in the sun, but Ariana and I ended up being led around a large lake at a fairly rapid pace. I have to admit that the lake, which was surrounded by trees, shrubs and picturesque planting, was a lovely place to stroll. However, warming temperatures and cumulative fatigue meant that after our circumnavigation I was ready for a rest. Ariana and Alison chatted, as I lay down, scrunched my eyes against the sun and let everything else drift by.

As things drifted by, I must have drifted off. The next thing I remember was someone nudging me in the ribs and my name being called over and over again. I woke, dazed and confused.

I hate being rudely awakened, so I wasn't in the best of moods. I wasn't quite sure about what was happening or where I was. However, I soon realised the gravity of the situation.

Things had changed. Times had changed. Tranquillity had drifted by.

I was still lying on the ground with Ariana and Alison close by, but we had company. We were surrounded by seven or eight bikers dressed in denim and leathers and smelling of patchouli oil. Granada's answer to the Hell's Angels looked both moody and menacing. They sat on their bikes with engines revving. They stared with the frightening intensity of butchers whose cars smell of blood. How on earth I hadn't woken up sooner, I'll never know.

'*Hijo de puta*,' shouted one particularly large biker, who looked and acted like the leader of the pack. I looked around, but I accurately guessed that he was talking to me. After his initial accusation about my mother's choice of career and familiar connection, my parentage was repeatedly questioned before a whole torrent of abuse was hurled in my general direction. Chief Biker wasn't happy about the fact that I was with two girls, and he really wasn't happy about the fact that one of them was Spanish. I got the distinct impression that he'd been to too many right-wing meetings and not enough anger management classes.

Ariana looked worried, but she reacted in typical style. Unbowed and angry, she told Chief Biker to fuck off and when he got there to fuck off again. Fortunately, she shouted in English. Unfortunately, the biker appeared to understand English vernacular. Bike chains appeared, wrapped around fists, some of which were already encased by knuckledusters. I stood up, not to stand my ground, but because I didn't know what else to do and I didn't want to be run over. I couldn't think of anything useful or pithy to say, so I repeated Ariana's battle cry and prepared myself for annihilation.

Engines revved, chains were gripped and the bikes began to circle. The smell of engine oil mingled with the smell of fear. The circle closed and I presumed that our end was neigh. As last stands go, this was going to be quick.

'*He llamado a la policía. He llamado a la policía*.'

An elderly lady appeared from over the horizon (or more accurately, from a small kiosk located close by). She shouted at the top of her voice as she ran towards us. Her voice echoed above the two-stroke cacophony. The bikers halted their advance. The cavalry had arrived. Chief Biker turned and spat in my general direction, before kickstarting his bike and roaring off. He was closely followed by his acolytes.

It transpired that the gang were frequent visitors to the park and frequent offenders. They regularly robbed, harassed and attacked tourists and locals alike. But, thanks to our grey-haired savour, the police were on their case. We thanked her and we thanked our lucky stars. Over the last couple of days, we'd jumped straight out of the frying pan and straight into the fire, but we'd survived – the flames had been extinguished. Things could only get better.

GRANADA
Second Thoughts

THIS IS NOW

If I had to choose, and it's an almost impossible choice, Granada would have to be my favourite Spanish city. It's a city that's full of character, life and marvellous memories. Geographically, culturally, architecturally, and in my case personally, Granada is the perfect mix of past and present. We all have a 'sense of place', even about places that we've never visited. Media representations, paintings, history, poetry and prose conjure up ideas, views and attitudes. Distant places can take on a familiar feel. Real lived experience of place, however, creates a stronger emotional attachment. This may be negative or positive, but if we connect we may develop a sense of belonging. Experience develops oneness. Our lives, or at least a part of them, become interlinked with the bricks and mortar of place. If we throw our arms around a city, thoroughly

and unreservedly embracing its uniqueness, then we may also absorb its very essence. If a place has importance for us then that place becomes important to us. I couldn't possibly imagine a world without Granada, and I can't imagine myself without my Granada experience. In short, part of me will forever belong to Granada, but part of Granada belongs to me.

Granada is the capital city of the province of Granada. Its site is an almost perfect spot in which to establish a settlement. Granada is located at the confluence of four rivers – the Beiro, the Darro, the Genil and the Monachil – at the point at which the Sierra Nevada mountains meet the fertile plain of the Vega. The mountains provide protection and a constant supply of water while the rich soil of the Vega provides productive agricultural land.

Unsurprisingly, Granada's favourable setting has attracted many different groups of settlers to set up home. Granada was first inhabited by native tribes in the prehistoric period: early Iberians named it Elibyrge. When the Romans arrived and colonised, they built their own city in the same location and called it Illiberis. After the decline and fall of the Roman Empire, and a period of uncertainty, the Moorish conquest of the region eventually led to the Berber, Zawi Ben Ziri, establishing an independent kingdom with Illiberis as its capital. At the same time, the local Jewish community established themselves on a hill close by. The hill was called Garnata, which probably meant 'hill of strangers'. This highland provided a good defensive position and was soon home to the ruling families of the area. The name of the hill, Garnata, could help to explain the origin of the place name Granada, but Granada is also Spanish for pomegranate: an abundant local fruit.

After the fall of Cordoba to Christian forces in 1236, Granada became the capital of the Emirate of Granada: the last Moorish stronghold in Spain. For the next 250 years, Granada was the beating heart of a powerful and self-sufficient kingdom; it was this period that saw the building of the Alhambra. Throughout this period, however, the Emirate of Granada came under increasing pressure from the Crown of Castile. In the late 15th century, the Christian Reconquista set its sights firmly on the city of Granada. The end of Moorish rule in the Iberian Peninsula was nigh. Following a military campaign led by Ferdinand and Isabella, Emir Muhammad XII (also known as Boabdil of Granada) surrendered the city in 1492.

Endings and beginnings are usually paired events. Tolerance and enlightenment were replaced by prejudice and ignorance. The Christian conquerors started to make significant changes to the appearance of the city in an attempt to hide its Muslim character; they also forced Jewish and Muslim residents to convert to Christianity.

Persecution of and against the Muslims and Jews took its toll. The city almost inevitably began to decline as a result. The Christian conquerors were persecuting the very people who were responsible for the city's wealth and grandeur. Granada would never be quite the same again.

A brief resurgence in fortunes did occur in the 17th century, but this was followed by further decline. Napoleon's occupation of the city in the early 19th century caused great damage and almost resulted in the complete destruction of the Alhambra: an attempt to blow up the whole palace complex was only thwarted when one valiant soldier removed the fuses from a vast quantity of explosives just before they were set to explode.

Railway links and tourism led to another brief resurgence in fortunes and some development in the late 19th century, but despite ideas to the contrary, things didn't get that much better. Granada may have been an urban area, but it was fast becoming a rural backwater. This sense of faded glory prevailed into the 20th century. Lorca argued that Granada's economic stagnation was due to its conservative, arrogant and cool bourgeoisie, who together with the military and the clerics discouraged industrial development and innovation. Liberal ideas and ideology were an anathema to the ruling classes of the city, who rose up and unleashed a blood bath at the outbreak of the Civil War. An estimated 7,000 Liberals and Republicans were assassinated, including (as we have seen) Lorca himself.

The post-Franco era has been kinder to the city. In recent years, Granada has been more successful in its attempts to regenerate and revive its fortunes. Investment, modernisation and development have brought new businesses, new life and new visitors to the city. Granada has grown as a consequence and modern architecture points towards a new-found confidence. Granada's future looks brighter than it has for a long time.

We arrived in the city by bus, always a joyous alternative to the congestion and confusion engendered by private transport. If truth be told, it would have been tricky to arrive by car. Granada is surrounded by a tortuously complicated one-way system and if you manage to negotiate your way through it, you are faced with a further problem – private vehicles are banned from the city centre. CCTV monitors movement and cars entering the heart of the city are photographed and fined. There are, however, some exceptions. If you're booked to stay in a central hotel, you're exempt from any fines. Hotels pass on vehicle registration details to the transport police and any cars identified by this process are allowed free passage.

We were booked to stay at Hotel Comfort Dauro 2. First and second impressions were more than favourable. The rooms were clean, cool and spacious. The location was perfect. The cathedral and Royal Chapel were only a stone's throw away, as were many other historic sites, some fabulous bars and some glorious eateries. Our room overlooked Calle Navas, a narrow, busy street packed full of tapas bars and restaurants. You could smell the food, taste the excitement and feel the buzz. We couldn't wait to get out and about. We wanted to experience all that Granada had to offer.

Hunger guided our first exploration of the city, but we didn't explore for very long and we didn't venture too far. In the same street as the hotel we discovered Los Diamantes, a tapas bar specialising in seafood: it was a discovery that invited immediate occupation. Unlike our usual tapas bars, Los Diamantes was modern, white-tiled and brightly lit, but just like our usual tapas bars the place was crowded, warm and welcoming. There were hardly any tables and chairs and there was little standing room, but the smell of freshly fried fish set us salivating. The bar has a simple concept: cold beer and delicious seafood, served quickly and efficiently. We shouted our order, raising our voices to make ourselves heard above the general din of dining. We were rewarded by ice cold drinks and piping hot *boquerones* (fried anchovies). The cheap beer and the free food were fantastic. The perfectly crisp batter and its succulent content may have been complimentary, but it was worthy of compliment. The temptation for one drink to become two was overwhelming, but we steadfastly resisted temptation. We had a city to discover, or to rediscover in my case.

We continued heading along Calle Navas until we arrived at Plaza del Carmen. Our intention was to visit the tourist office and obtain a street map, but we were momentarily distracted by the ongoing construction of a large stage in the beautifully ornate square. We wondered what was planned for later in the evening and pondered the past as we admired the sculptured space. It was here, in the Plaza del Carmen, that workers massed at the outbreak of the Civil War in support of the Republic. Reacting to rumours and counter-rumours,

Republican supporters gathered outside the town hall in a show of strength. Initially uncertain about the intentions of the locally based troops, the unarmed workers were forced to stand down as artillery pieces and machine guns were brought into the plaza to threaten the crowd. It hadn't taken the military long to reveal their true colours. As we pondered the future and thought about the past, the temptation for one drink to become two finally overwhelmed our steadfastness. In our defence, it must be said that a big part of discovering any city is discovering its bars and restaurants. Our next destination was a second lunch stop. Once again, we disregarded Jose's Law, as we stepped inside La Cueva de 1900. The tapas bar and restaurant was another modern-looking one; this time part of a chain. However, despite outward appearances, the inside of the bar was traditionally styled, the clientele were local, the food was good and the beer was cold.

Temporarily full and currently satiated we headed towards the centre of the city, and I headed towards my past. We strolled along Calle Reyes Catolicos with the casual attitude of the truly contented. We ventured into some of the elegant shops that lined our way before arriving at Plaza Nueva and Plaza Santa Ana. Plaza Nueva, or New Public Square, brought back some old memories.

If I'd been asked about the area before my return, I wouldn't have been able to describe Plaza Nueva, but it immediately had a familiar feel. I recognised the structure and shape of the surrounding buildings and I felt a oneness with the space. The square had changed, but at the same time it had a comforting similarity. The pavements were more crowded and cluttered, and everything appeared to more colourful than I remembered. Bright awnings, multi-hued umbrellas and a vast array of tables and chairs filled the immediate area. My memories of the space were more monochrome. I'd pictured the area in black and white. Perhaps we don't dream in colour? Perceptions aside, I could picture the past and I was transported back in time. A young couple sat at a round table: talking, laughing and drinking, they were oblivious to the past or the future and were unquestionably living in the now. They appeared from the shadows of memory without any conscious thought and fleetingly took on a solid reality. Oblivious of everyone else and invisible to anyone else, they were clear to me. I looked closer and saw their faces, their passion, their hope and their optimism. But as I stared they disappeared, fading out as the present screamed in. I couldn't see their future.

'*Yo te acuerda, oh mi corazón.*'

'What are you looking at?' said Tom. 'Right now, I'm looking at my family and thinking that everything happens for a reason.' Tom looked confused, so I continued. 'Trust to fate. Things have a habit of working out for the best.' Tom looked doubtful, but it was time to move on.

As we moved on, La Iglesias de San Gil y Santa Ana increasingly dominated the scene. Built on the site of a former mosque and incorporating its minaret, the picturesque church was a Mudejar prototype. The past had been used to shape the future. The impressive building sits next to the River Darro, just at the point at which the river disappears underground. I'm sure that the interior of the building is worthy of exploration, but we investigated some temples of commerce instead. The narrow Carrera del Darro, which borders the river, is home to a number of Moroccan shops. The colourful and eclectic emporiums sold mosaic-style glass lamps and lampshades, delicate tea sets, chess sets, elegant dresses, slippers, beautiful rugs, jewellery, leather bags and a whole variety of other goods. The shopkeepers were masters of their trade: warm and entertaining, friendly and funny; we bought more than we intended or needed.

After our unplanned shopping excursion, we headed back towards the Capilla Real de Granada (Royal Chapel of Granada). Located next to the cathedral, Capilla Real is home to the tombs of Isabella and Ferdinand, their daughter Joanna the Mad, her husband Philip I of Castile, and also Miguel da Paz. The Catholic monarchs, Isabella and Ferdinand, chose their own resting place. They decided that the conquest of Granada was of such great importance that their remains should forever remain within the city.

Most historians trace the beginnings of modern Spain back to the union of Isabella and Ferdinand. Their marriage effectively united the kingdoms of Castile and Aragon, but the Catholic monarchs ruled with a degree of independence and their original kingdoms retained regional laws and governments for many years. The significance of their joint reigns cannot, however, be disputed. For better or worse, they presided over the dawn of a new modern age: the completion of the Reconquista, the discovery of the Americas, the expulsion of the Jews and Muslims and the infamous Spanish Inquisition. They also ensured long-term stability for Spain, by ensuring that their children married, if not well, then politically advantageously. Two of their daughters were married to members of the Portuguese royal family; their only son was married to Margaret of Austria to strengthen links with the Hapsburgs (one of the most influential and important royal houses in Europe); their youngest daughter, Catherine, was married to Arthur Prince of Wales, before becoming the first wife of Arthur's brother, Henry VIII of England; last, but not least, Joanna the Mad married Philip the Handsome, who was the son of the Holy Roman Emperor. The Holy Roman Empire was potentially Europe's greatest state: it was composed of a varying combination of lands in western and central Europe, ruled over by Frankish kings. The Holy Roman Emperor was an important friend to have. Philip was also a Hapsburg. The future of Spain as a nation state was secure; however, the mental state of Joanna was less secure. Besotted with a philandering husband, involuntarily embroiled in political machinations, heir to the throne and heir to some dodgy genes, Joanna was a tortured soul. Modern historians view Joanna more favourably and kindly than some past historians, but most agree that her delicate mental state was pushed to breaking point by the death of her husband when he was only twenty-eight. As a child Joanna was considered to be highly intelligent, but she may have suffered from depression or possibly schizophrenia. After the death of her husband, stories spread that she would open his coffin every night to embrace his corpse. Whatever the truth of her mental state, rumours and stories didn't help her case. Joanna spent most of the rest of her long life confined to the Royal Convent of Santa Clara in Tordesillas, while others ruled in her place. Joanna's is a sad story: she was a victim of her own melancholy, but also of the political ambition of those around her.

Joanna the (perhaps not so) Mad's trials and tribulations link to another sad story, that of the early death of the Infante Miguel da Paz, Prince of Portugal. Born in Zaragoza, Miguel da Paz was the son of Isabella of Aragon and Manuel I of Portugal; he was the grandson of Ferdinand and Isabella. His death, after that of his mother and just before his second birthday, dashed all hopes of uniting the Iberian kingdoms under an Iberian king. His death meant that Joanna became heir to the Spanish throne. Miguel da Paz's small lead coffin sadly sits next to those of Isabella and Ferdinand, and Joanna and Philip, in the crypt of the Capilla Real.

The Capilla Real is exquisitely designed. The tomb effigies of the former monarchs are intricately and delicately carved. The lead tombs under the crypt are plain, but emotive and thought-provoking. Experiencing a real sense of history, we headed into an adjoining room and explored a small museum. We were amazed to see some original banners and flags which had been carried into the final battles against the Moors by the armies of Ferdinand and Isabella. Not for the first time today, the past, perhaps bizarrely, seemed very much alive.

In an attempt to keep the past alive, we decided to visit the cathedral, before returning to the hotel for a quick siesta. The Cathedral of the Incarnation was a haven of cool and calm. The surprisingly light and airy interior was an amazing place to be. Soaring vertical columns, high ceilings, beautiful domes, an elaborate altar and fabulous carvings transported us to yet another new reality. I don't usually use them, but an audio guide included within the admission price added to our enjoyment and piqued our interest. The history of the building and the stories behind the numerous works of art and reliquaries were clearly expounded and explained.

History was all around us. Spain is a country with a rich and interesting past, but it's also a country which lives for the present: it's very much alive. One of the real joys of Spain is that there always seems to be something going on. As we left the cathedral we were treated to the free spectacle of some flamenco. Two female performers took it in turns to dance to the recorded strains of some intricate guitar playing. The first dancer was small, dark and passionately balletic. The second dancer was tall, blond and statuesque: hers was an athletic performance full of clipped power and dramatic posturing. A third male performer didn't dance, but he certainly looked the part. Dressed in Cuban-heeled boots, high-waisted black trousers, red shirt and black waistcoat, with jet black hair swept back into a ponytail, he was the epitome of a Gitano *bailaor*. He might not have danced, but he certainly posed; his sheer presence was a performance.

That Was Then

It was late, but not that late for Spain. We'd had a few drinks, but we were well practised. We headed along Carrera del Darro before turning left, heading uphill and then turning right towards Sacromonte: the traditional neighbourhood of the Granadian Gitanos, or Gypsies. Our destination was a regular haunt – a nightclub in a cave house.

Carved into the solid but soft rock of the area, cave houses epitomise Sacromonte. The mostly underground houses come in a variety of forms. We walked past houses that were more cave than house: often just simple openings in a cliff face, concealing inner spaces with few facilities or amenities. Other houses offered the full facade of traditional houses, with front doors, windows and gardens, concealing a subterranean world of cave bedrooms and sittings rooms hidden just out of sight. Plainly in sight, families sat outside their dwellings; sometimes smoking, sometimes drinking and sometimes eating, but always talking and smiling. We'd been warned to watch out for our wallets and our skins, but you shouldn't prejudge people, you should take people as you find them. I've always found the Spanish to be warm and friendly, but when it comes to their Gypsy neighbours and Gitano countrymen, some of them can be quite prejudiced.

We ignored the prejudice and we sensed the pride of the local people. The area looked impoverished, but it felt socially cohesive and emotionally prosperous. Sacromonte has always been a home for those on the fringes of society, those living just enough for the city. Cave houses were originally built by and for the disadvantaged and the poor. But the tradition of cave house dwelling predates the arrival of the Gypsies, who migrated into the area from India in the late 14th century. Before their arrival, Sacromonte was a Muslim and then a Moroscos neighbourhood. It was the expulsion of the Muslims, and then the Moroscos, that led to the area becoming a predominantly Gypsy neighbourhood. Today, the tenure of this ethic enclave is being challenged: artists, artisans, bohemians and property speculators are moving in.

We kept moving on.

With a singleness of purpose, we headed along Camino del Sacromonte, successfully resisting all requests to step inside this or that flamenco bar. The offers of authentic entertainment were less authentic than the entertainment offered in many of the side streets. Our goal was our nightclub, and our aim was true. Entrance was gained via a traditional front door and patio, which concealed a unique interior. The ground floor was an irregular network of interconnected caves. The caves varied in size and shape: some were dedicated dance floors, others were slightly smaller and quieter 'chill out' zones, one was a very crowded and busy bar, but all reverberated to the sound of the crowd, quite literally so – The Human League, and the voice of Phil Oakey, swirled and echoed around the cavernous building.

We felt at home in this home for the generally disaffected – 'indie kids' and 'students'. We headed for the dance floor and danced as if our lives depended upon it. Arms pumped, feet tapped, heads snapped and bodies gyrated as sweat dripped from ourselves and the low ceiling. The Human League faded out as Aztec Camera's 'Walk Out to Winter' faded in. I smiled. To a large extent, this is what I lived for. This was 12" dance floor mix heaven. Just when I thought things couldn't get any better, the crisp, sparkling, jingly-jangly guitar of Johnny Marr announced the 'New York' mix of 'This Charming Man'. I felt as alive, if not more alive than I'd ever been. I was that 'jumped-up pantry boy', but I could go out tonight and I didn't know my place.

In the words of another song, 'I could have danced all night', but three songs in a row – well, two and half to be precise – had worn me out. The beat faded out and a raging thirst kicked in. We headed towards the bar. As I squeezed through the crowd and tried to catch the barman's eye, someone else caught my ear. 'Hey, Bank Robber, you murdered my song.' I turned. I was surprised to hear an English voice and I was even more surprised when I saw the owner of the voice. An imposing, slightly angry-looking character, dressed in black T-shirt and jeans, gazed down at me. The last time I'd seen the same face gazing down at me, it had been staring out from a poster on my bedroom wall. I was in the presence of rock royalty. I was in the presence of Joe Strummer, and apparently, I'd been in his presence before.

I didn't know what to say or do. I mumbled an apology about my guitar playing and singing. He smiled a half smile as he ambled away from the bar. 'Bloody hell. Joe Strummer!' I should have made more of the moment, but surprisingly, and even more bizarrely, I would get a second chance.

Ariana was far less surprised to see Joe Strummer than I was. Apparently, Joe had a Spanish girlfriend and he'd been living in Granada for a couple of months. Apparently, we had a couple of things in common. Overcome by emotion and overexcited, but too overawed and too self-conscious to pursue a conversation with one of my idols, I headed up some steps to a raised terrace. The raised terrace contained another bar, which was fortunate, because I'd forgotten to buy any drinks. The terrace also contained another dance floor: both bar and dance floor offered fantastic views across to the Alhambra.

A good night had turned into a great night, and had the potential to become a fantastic night.

Granada was calling.

THIS IS NOW

We felt both rested and revived, which was just as well because the night and the city beckoned – Granada was still calling. We emerged from the hotel with few plans, but with an appetite for aimless adventure. We sauntered back along Calle Navas, and stopped for a first pre-prandial drink at El Tabernaculo. The small bar is dedicated to Santa Semana. Everywhere we looked there were posters and prayer cards of Jesus and the Virgin Mary. It was an immersive religious and epicurean experience – incense and arias filled the air while the free tapas were a revelation.

Beginning to feel too close to the divine for comfort, I started to experience a personal urge to confess – but we didn't have all night, so we moved on. Stepping back out onto the street, the sound of religious songs was replaced by the sound of *Strictly Come Dancing*. My urge to confess diminished, replaced by an urge to dance. A Cha-cha-cha faded into a Rumba, which increased in volume as we headed towards the Plaza del Carmen.

Two keyboard players performed on the now fully constructed stage. The area immediately in front of the stage had been set aside as a dance floor. The dance floor was bordered by rows of wooden chairs, most of which were occupied by perched pensioners. Three couples danced, while one dapper and debonair gentleman circled the edge of the dance floor, stopping every now and again to exchange pleasantries with the ladies in the audience. The dancers may have been elderly, but they certainly knew how to dance. Dressed 'up to the nines', men in smart shirts and ties danced with ladies in fancy frocks. Light on their feet, the burden of their years appeared to become irrelevant as the magic of the music and the moment took over. Once again, I noticed the 'circling' gentleman. He was slightly unsteady on his feet, but he was steadfast in his ambition. He bowed before speaking to one particularly glamorous elderly lady. She smiled. He took her by the hand and led her to the dance floor. They swirled and twirled, his formerly halting gait now replaced by energetic and vigorous footwork. The years fell away from him. He smiled. I think he thought he'd pulled. Perhaps he had?

'This is how to grow old,' I thought. Elegantly, and hopefully somewhat disgracefully. Dancing, smiling and flirting, out in the open air rather than locked away in solitary confusion with only a TV and a microwave meal for company. The Spanish know how to live and how to die. Don't fade away, radiate.

As we continued to watch, more couples took to the dance floor. A change in tempo, from Rumba to Disco, allowed for more universal participation. I grabbed Tania by the hand, the boys put their heads in their hands. Life (I reminded myself) shouldn't be a spectator sport. We headed for the dance floor and danced, maybe not as if our lives depended upon it, but with suitably enthusiastic commitment. Arms pumped, feet tapped, heads snapped and bodies gyrated as we embarrassed our children and possibly ourselves. I could have danced all night, but I'm not sure that I would have been allowed to: it was time to move on.

We wandered towards another square – Plaza Bib Rambla, or as it's sometimes known, Plaza de las Flores. The charming square was filled with cafes and shops, which inhabited the ground floors of some grandiose four- and five-storey buildings. The fact that many of the buildings varied in colour added to the overall beauty of the scene. In the centre of the square, fenced off from the public, sat an ornate baroque fountain. Grotesque figures, spouting water from their mouths, held aloft a statue of Neptune. The whole area was shaded by lime trees. The impressive square was more 'touristy' than some others that we have visited. The 'touristy' feel was reflected in the prices that some of the cafes were charging, but it was still definitely worth a visit.

Today, the Plaza Bib Rambla is a picture of calm enchantment, but in the past, it was the scene of some quite repugnant practices. The area was home to *autos-da-fé* (trials of faith).

The Spanish Inquisition lasted for an extraordinary 350 years, from 1478 until 1834. The idea behind the Inquisition (which was originally sanctioned by the Pope) was to root out non-believers. Despite initial promises to the contrary, Catholicism was seen as the one and only permissible faith. Ferdinand and Isabella wanted to 'purify the people of Spain'. The Inquisition was met with resistance, but the Catholic monarchs established permanent trials and an investigative bureaucracy, the likes of which and the scale of which had never been seen before.

The now infamous Tomas de Torquemada was given the role of Inquisitor General. He established the Inquisition's procedural rules. People could be accused of wrongdoing by the general population, but they had no right to know who their accusers were. If they admitted to any wrongdoings and turned in any other wrongdoers or converted to Catholicism, they would be released or given a short prison sentence. However, if they refused to cooperate, then they would be either publicly executed (sometimes by being burnt at the stake) or sentenced to life imprisonment. The fate of the accused was determined at an *auto-da-fé*. These were large, solemn occasions, designed to instil fear and respect into not just the accused, but also into those who watched the events unfold.

Two processions would have converged in the square in which we now stood: one would have brought the accused from wherever they were being held, and the other would have been made up of the local clergy. Hooded penitents and the unrepentant would have awaited their fate. Events usually lasted from dawn until dusk. It was horrific to think that people could and would have been sentenced to death and burnt alive in this very location.

We took a final look around Plaza Bib Rambla, before leaving both the square and Spain behind us. We stepped from the square into Calle Ermita: it felt like we were stepping into Morocco – Marrakech was calling. Middle Eastern shops lined the street. Not for the first time today, we ended up buying things that we didn't really need.

From Calle Ermita, we headed back towards the cathedral. The first thing I noticed was something that I hadn't noticed on our first visit. The name 'Jose Antonio Primo de Rivera' had been neatly etched into the solid stone of the building. The graffiti (for that's what it is) dates back to the early days of the Civil War, but the name had recently been splattered with red paint. The red paint had dripped down the side of the building and dried into what looked like five rivulets of blood. Jose Primo de Rivera, the founder of the right-wing Falangist party, was killed very early on in the Spanish Civil War; it is said that his supporters heralded him as a martyr and scratched his name onto every cathedral in Spain. This poignant reminder of Spain's bloody past was all too visible in the present. If the graffiti was originally intended as a memorial, why is it still in place today? Jose Primo de Rivera has blood on his hands. Graffiti means to scratch. This was clear, literal evidence of a previously mentioned and uncomfortable truth – if you scratch the surface and delve into the past, Spain is still a divided nation.

It was time to get back to some more comfortable truths – love conquers all and love is stronger than death. Well, you have to believe in something. The Spanish appear to be in love with love, but marriage, however, is a different matter. There has been a steady decline in the percentage of people marrying in Spain since the 1960s. In 2015, only 3.4 persons per thousand got married (in 1960, the rate was 7.8 persons per thousand) and only 22 per cent of those who married got married in a religious ceremony. Recession, apathy and a commitment to mortgage rather than marriage appear to be some of the factors that underlie this recent trend. When the Spanish do marry, however, they inevitably do so in style.

As I contemplated the legacy of the Spanish Civil War, we stumbled upon a lavish wedding ceremony – love was in the air.

Situated next to Granada Cathedral is the Iglesia del Sagrario (Church of the Tabernacle). It's often overlooked, but it hadn't been overlooked by the happy couple who emerged from the building as we gate-crashed the tail end of their ceremony. The bride and groom were met with an avalanche of rice. They both looked immaculate. The bride wore a traditional white lace dress; veil removed, her ecstatic face beamed with happiness. The bridegroom was suited and booted; his handsome features radiated love and pride. The guests were an impressive bunch as well. Elegant figures in elegant dresses and sharp suits thronged the main protagonists. Spain has one of the highest divorce rates in Europe, but at this moment in time it looked like love would last. The romantic optimist in me hoped that it would.

As more and more guests emerged from the church, we took the opportunity to step inside. The exterior of the Iglesia del Sagrario is rather austere, but the interior was as dazzling as the bride and groom. Built in Baroque style, it's modelled on the Basilica of St Peter in Rome. The ornate altar of marble and polished wood was festooned with flowers; the floral fantasy took our breath away. An hemispherical dome covered the chancel and immense columns decorated with large statues of angels supported a larger dome above the nave. Small chapels, monuments and some confessional boxes lined the sides and the back of the church. Overawed but underdressed, we mingled with the departing guests. This was a building and a moment to savour.

After savouring the moment, we decided that it was time to savour some food. We headed towards one of the oldest bars in Granada – Bodegas Castaneda.

Tiled walls, wooden screens and oak barrels decorated the delightfully atmospheric bar. It looked like standing room only, and it was. We managed to find a vacant table in a small alcove, but there weren't any chairs. Standing tall, we ordered two boards of assorted tapas – one hot and one cold – both were delicious.

After rounding off our meal with a couple of glasses of chilled red wine, we decided to head up towards the Mirador St Nicolas: I would try to resist the urge to busk. Almost immediately, we found ourselves transported back to a Spanish version of Morocco – cafes, hookah bars, tea shops and restaurants with a North African flavour lined the cobbled streets. The streets were far busier than I remembered. Crowds of people had had the same idea as us. One thing that's certain is that you'll never be lonely if you use a Lonely Planet guide. Times had changed.

Most of the voices that surrounded us spoke English – maybe with an American or an Australian accent, but they spoke English just the same. The days of Granada and its environs being universally and uniquely Spanish had gone. Tourism may have taken over, but the Albaicin still had a unique charm.

A Spanish family sat outside their home, playing with a tiny puppy – passers-by were invited to admire and 'pet' this new edition to their family. A guitarist entertained a small crowd on some steps outside an elegant church – his efforts drew appreciative applause. Customers talked, drank and laughed as they watched the world go by sitting outside Cafe 4 Gatos – we joined them for a while. Grilled openings in doorways revealed picturesque inner courtyard gardens – well watered and green, they provided a contrast to the otherwise desiccated barrio. Narrow streets twisted and turned as they climbed ever higher – gaps in between buildings offered tantalising views of the mighty, majestic and brightly illuminated Alhambra – the golden palace looked ethereal as it floated on high.

Everything about our evening was confirming my love of Granada.

The final short climb up to the Mirador San Nicolas was a steep slog, but the views fully justified the effort involved – if there is a more magical place with a better view, then please let me know. We edged our way through the crowds to a low wall which concealed a steep drop – it was here, once upon a time, that Joe Strummer famously posed. It's the view of the Alhambra, backed by the Sierra Nevada mountains, that first captures the eye and the imagination (the palace looks even more mighty and majestic from this most favoured of viewpoints), then your eyes move to the right and the whole city of Granada, sparkling and twinkling in the twilight, stretches out before you. The views merge, together they complete a perfect scene – old, new, low-rise, high-rise, palaces and pavements, street lights and floodlights, rooftops and ruins, historic, modern, captivating, shimmering and vibrant – it's simply stunning – all you can do is stop and stare.

That Was Then

Firmly ensconced on the terrace, we gazed across to the Alhambra in a state of 'joint' ecstasy. Music played as people chatted and danced, but the view was all – everything else was a peripheral distraction. Perched on its own hill, a crowning glory, the ancient palace filled our eyes, our hearts and our thoughts. The moment was simply magical.

THIS IS NOW

I couldn't stop staring at the view – I was transfixed. I turned my head slowly, again and again, as my eyes took in the buildings of the palace, the Generalife and the city streets of modern Granada. The view was as magical now as it had been then.

Considering the size of the crowd, we'd been fortunate to find a spot next to the low wall, so we made the most of our moment. We gazed in shared wonder, but lost ourselves in splendid isolation before discussing the moment and then posing for a family photo. The area buzzed with energy and excitement. The Mirador is so much more than a just a viewpoint: guitarists played, artists painted and street traders (perhaps not unsurprisingly) traded.

We traded our thoughts as we turned our backs to the view. We made our way back through the crowd and entered the relative sanctuary of Iglesia San Nicolas. The church, which looks spectacular from the outside, is little more than an empty shell. Set alight by Republican supporters in the Civil War, the church is ready for restoration. The Albaicin held out for the Republic before being shelled into submission by fascist forces. The now dilapidated church was an early victim of the conflict, but its former glory is still discernible. A friendly and informative custodian answered William's questions about the history of the church and the area before inviting us all to climb to the top of the bell tower. There's normally a charge, but today admission was free – the custodian appeared to be rewarding William's historical curiosity.

We climbed ever higher and higher. We huddled around the bells and gazed once again upon the Alhambra and the city streets of Granada. Our tower-top eyrie provided yet another spectacular viewpoint.

After descending, we re-entered the packed Mirador, before walking into an adjacent living, breathing and praying mosque. The Grand Mosque of Granada is the first mosque to be opened in Spain since the Reconquista. Completed in 2003, the mosque is a spiritual home to 500 Muslims. Its opening was not without controversy, but let's hope that it's a sign and a symbol of religious freedom, tolerance and understanding. The mosque itself preaches the mantra of harmonious coexistence. We felt very welcome and the extensive gardens offered a space to all for quiet reflection. The beautifully ornate and tranquil gardens also offered yet more spectacular views towards the Alhambra. That a mosque should now overlook the ancient Moorish palace has, in itself, a clear spiritual significance – let's hope that it's the dawn of a new age of mutuality – it certainly feels right.

Turning left, we headed towards the Gitano quarter – our destination a former nightclub in a cave house. Guided by Google, it was time to rediscover Sacromonte. The area hadn't changed as much as I thought it might have done, but the nightclub was now a flamenco bar. The area was all a little quieter and a little cleaner and apparently it's much safer, but it had a familiar feel. People still sat outside their homes and their homes were clearly caves. We passed restaurants and abandoned excavations. We stopped for a drink at a bar and the boys marvelled at the roughly carved and exquisitely decorated inner rooms. Whitewashed walls and colourful wall hangings couldn't, however, mask the overriding aroma of damp.

We sat outside the bar and watched the world go by. Tourists pulled cases, families sought food and drink as revellers sought entertainment; all were silhouetted by the moon and the floodlit Alhambra. Something, however, was missing. Where were all the locals? Perhaps the area had changed far more than I'd initially thought.

A young man walked past – he looked familiar. Hands in pockets, he sashayed down the street. Another shadow of the past? I looked towards Tania and the boys. Let the past lie. The here and now and the future is all that really matters – it's all that we can control. We gathered our thoughts and then gathered ourselves before heading back to our hotel. The young man was heading in an opposite direction – my shadow in vain – missed chances but no regrets.

That Was Then

'If you remember the '60s, you really weren't there' is a much-used quote. It describes the post-war, post-austerity cultural explosion that took place in much of the western world in the 1960s – Spain, however, lagged a little behind. 'If you lived in the '80s and remember it, then you didn't live it' is a popular saying used to describe the explosion in creativity, in fashion, cinema, theatre, music, sexuality, nightlife and narcotic life that took place in Spain during the 1980s. Franco's vision of a traditional Spain meant that laws were put in place to restrict drinking, drugs and late-night entertainment. It wasn't exactly prohibition, but much was prohibited. Franco's death marked the beginning of a hedonistic countercultural revolution. Widely believed to have started in Madrid in 1980, 'La Movida', as it became known, coincided with the beginnings of economic growth and the emergence of a new Spanish identity after the death of Franco and the decline of Francoism.

La Movida was an unplanned phenomenon, characterised by freedom of expression, a transgression of the taboos imposed by the Franco regime, the use of recreational drugs, punk/new wave culture, a spirit of freedom and sexual revolution. Everything went, and anything counted – perhaps it was more style than substance, but it was real, and it gave us Pedro Almodovar, to name but one. The movement may have started in Madrid, but it soon spread to other cities throughout Spain, including Granada.

True to the spirit of the times, we rolled another Rizla as we continued to survey the scene. Our insights were magnified by retrospective meanderings. Shortly afterwards, counterfeit to the spirit of the times and the countercultural revolution, we were admonished and evicted from the club. La Movida was obviously somewhere else.

THIS IS NOW

One of the real joys of any holiday is the fact that you can switch off your alarm clock. Whilst I understand that the function of an alarm clock is to get people out of bed, I despise its efficiency of purpose. Apart from announcing the start of another working day, an alarm clock that interrupts your sleep can damage your memories, your ability to learn, your mood and temper, your relationships with other people, your ability to focus and your overall intellectual performance. It was somewhat disappointing, therefore, that in the morning we were rudely awakened by the annoying beeping of a very insistent and horribly familiar mechanical demon – silence was broken.

'Why the early start?' you may well ask. Well, we were off to visit the Alhambra. Now one of the most visited historical sites in the world, tickets needed to be booked well in advance. We hoped that an early visit would afford us the opportunity to avoid the worst of the crowds and the worst of the blistering heat which the Alhambra's elevated and somewhat exposed position can often deliver. In August, visitor numbers can approach 10,000 per day and temperatures can approach 40° Celsius.

The Alhambra Palace was originally built as a small fortress in 889. It was constructed in its present style by the Moorish Nasrid emirs in the 13th and 14th centuries. They extended the original fortress, in a most spectacular fashion, into a palace complex. The palace takes its name from the Arabic, *al-qala'a al-hamra*, or Red Palace, even though the original building was painted white. The name comes from the region's red clay.

The Alhambra's location, right at the top of the largely inaccessible Al-Sabika hill, overlooks the entire city of Granada – it's a great defensive position. Enemies would have struggled to reach the place, let alone gain entrance – we certainly did. Our tickets had been pre-booked on a credit card that no longer existed. The card had passed its sell-by date and it looked like we would pass our timed opportunity. The problem was the 'rules' which stated that you had to show the card that you had booked with in order to gain admittance. Eventually and fortunately, after an increasingly heated exchange, made increasingly uncomfortably by the presence of a not disinterested armed security guard, common sense and proof by way of an email trail prevailed. I couldn't help thinking that it was easier when you could just break in – not all in life is progress.

With our progression secured, we entered the palace complex. What can be said about the Alhambra that's not already been said? It's dazzling, breathtaking, eye-catching, it's the best-preserved medieval Moorish palace in the world – it's simply magnificent.

We walked through the Puerta de la Justica, a stunning horseshoe-shaped arch, perpendicularly angled to slow down invading armies. We explored the Alcazaba, and climbed up onto the Torre de la Vela, to enjoy the panoramic views of the Sierra Nevada. We entered the Palacio de Carlos V, a masterpiece of Renaissance art and design, which contrasts with the simply built Palacios Nazaries, designed not to compete with the creations of Allah, but to promote a divine presence and atmosphere. We marvelled at the Palacio de Los Leones, a courtyard surrounded by a low gallery supported by 124 white marble columns, which was originally the private quarters of the sultan, his family and his harem. We waited to take some pictures by the fountain of twelve lions, perhaps the most famous and certainly the most photographed image from inside the Alhambra complex. No one quite knows for sure, but the white marble lions may represent the twelve signs of the zodiac, or possibly the twelve hours of the day. When first designed, each and every hour one lion would produce water from its mouth. At the edge of the main fountain, which is encircled by the lions, there is a poem written by Ibn Zamrak. The poem praises the beauty of the fountain and the power of the lions, but it also describes the ingenious hydraulic system which is a key feature of the Alhambra itself.

'Water, water everywhere and many drops to drink.' The Ancient Mariner may have thirsted for fresh water, but in the Alhambra, it's found in abundance. Fountains, ponds, irrigation channels – the Alhambra is a celebration of H_2O. The sight and sound of water, a rare treasure in arid Andalusia, is never far away. Sound and vision indeed. Splashing into fountains, meandering through graceful channels, the celebration of water is integral to the Alhambra – as an art form it's the equal of the woodwork, ornate plaster and the ceramic tile of the palace itself.

From the main palace complex, we headed to the Genaralife, a Moorish villa with a beautiful courtyard surrounded by gardens which overlook the main Nasrid Palaces. Generalife, translates as 'the architects garden' or 'the best garden' or 'the high garden' – all translations are suitably apt and unarguably reflect reality. We walked past huge, sculptured hedges and perfectly planned planting. We walked next to an amphitheatre in a tree-lined hollow, where a stage and seating for outdoor concerts beguiled our imaginations. We climbed a water stairway, where channels of water cascaded down on either side of the steps punctuated by small fountains. We cooled our hands in the tantalising torrents. In the gardens of the Generalife in particular, the sound of running water was everywhere, in jets, fountains, pools and water channels. In the heat of the Spanish summer, this was the place where the Moorish kings came to relax and feel the cooler mountain air, serenaded by the music of running water. In the Muslim faith, Paradise is referred to as an oasis – a water garden full of fragrant blossoms. The Generalife is a place where you can clearly sense a little piece of heaven on earth.

The Generalife and the Alhambra have featured heavily in literature, most notably in Washington Irving's *Tales of the Alhambra* (1832), a book which I bought and read on my first visit to Spain. The American writer lived in the Alhambra while writing the book, which went on to introduce the, by then, rundown site to Western audiences. It's hard to imagine today, but for many years the Alhambra was left, abandoned and unloved, to quietly decay. It became a home to beggars, squatters, tramps and thieves; those on the fringes of society. Today, the Alhambra has been restored to match its original glory, and it has fully recaptured the imagination and interest of travellers. It may be busy, bustling and packed, but it's still magnificent. However, as we started heading downhill and away from the palace complex, I couldn't help but be thankful that I had once visited the Alhambra, without the crowds, under cover of the night, out of season and out of time.

We were running out of time, which inevitable speeds up when you're on holiday. Why is it that when you work, the hours and the minutes adopt a slower rhythm, but when you're on holiday time's arrow flies swiftly forwards? We still had much that we wanted to see and do, but perhaps illogically surmised that if we took our time, time might slow down. It was time to potter and wander and watch the world go by.

We drifted from shop to bar to restaurant and back again. I relived my youth. I sat outside cafes, chatting, drinking and just watching. Sometimes there is a real joy to be had in a life lived slowly and aimlessly – sometimes it's important to be idle. For a while at least, the pavement can be paradise. We enjoyed some tasty tapas and then slowly wandered back towards the 'Gran Via' – elegant, neoclassical buildings lined the thoroughfare. There is so much to enjoy and appreciate in Granada, that aimless wanderings usually reap rich rewards. We discovered so little, but so much. A second-hand clothes shop – nearly new but totally on trend; a poster shop, playing The Smiths and The Cure at full volume; a small square with a big presence; street entertainers, public art, street sculpture, history, people and an ice cream shop, Los Italianos, whose *helados* were to die for.

We headed back to the hotel and then drifted out again. Afternoon drifted into evening as we drifted along. A return to Los Diamantas proved that sometimes things are as good as the first time. A return to the Mirador San Nicolas and the Iglesia San Nicolas confirmed the point – the sun set as the views transfixed and transfigured. A night-time exploration of the Albaicin revealed floodlit ancient buildings, more Moorish arches, more 'Moorish' food, hidden squares, free tapas – potatoes and onions and paella – more *guitaristas*, more drinks, Moroccan-style fruit tea, more experiences and more memories. Life doesn't get much better than this. I was at one with Granada and I was at one with the past.

The following morning, we realised that our time in Granada had almost completely run out – the bus timetable provided the simple and inconvenient truth of the matter. I mentioned previously that there was still much that we wanted to see and do, but if truth be told, after the success of our more or less aimless wanderings of the night before, we knew that we would be happy to spend the morning just experiencing Granada for itself. However, in amongst our unplanned excursions, there was one thing that I'd planned to do, one thing that I wanted to do, one specific place that I was determined to visit – a pilgrimage of sorts. Fortunately, Tania and the boys were happy to accompany me.

Our destination was a small square situated to the south of the Alhambra. It took us a while to find it. With its white walls, reddish sand, pine trees, carved drinking fountain and spectacular views of the Sierra Nevada, the Placeta Joe Strummer is a memorial to The Clash's frontman.

Strummer was introduced to Granada by Esperanza Romero, a former fellow squatter who he had once shared a house with in London. Her sister, Paloma, would become Joe's girlfriend. Introduced to not only Granada, but to the culture of Andalusia, Lorca and stories of the Civil War, Strummer's interest and his songwriting was sparked and inspired. Strummer namechecked both Lorca and Granada in the 1979 song 'Spanish Bombs', which was released on

The Clash's *London Calling* album; not only was he inspired by Lorca, but he once tried to find and dig up the poet's grave.

Spanish songs in Andalucia
The shooting sites in the days of '39
Oh, please, leave the ventana open
Federico Lorca is dead and gone
Bullet holes in the cemetery walls
The black cars of the Guardia Civil
Spanish bombs on the Costa Rica
I'm flying in on a DC 10 tonight

Spanish bombs, yo te quiero infinito
yo te acuerda oh mi corazón
Spanish bombs, yo te quiero infinito
yo te acuerda oh mi corazón

Spanish weeks in my disco casino
The freedom fighters died upon the hill
They sang the red flag
They wore the black one
But after they died it was Mockingbird Hill
Back home the buses went up in flashes
The Irish tomb was drenched in blood
Spanish bombs shatter the hotels
My senorita's rose was nipped in the bud

Spanish bombs, yo te quiero infinito
yo te acuerda oh mi corazón
Spanish bombs, yo te quiero infinito
yo te acuerda oh mi corazón

The hillsides ring with "Free the people"
Or can I hear the echo from the days of '39?
With trenches full of poets

The ragged army, fixin' bayonets to fight the other line
Spanish bombs rock the province
I'm hearing music from another time
Spanish bombs on the Costa Brava
I'm flying in on a DC 10 tonight

Spanish bombs, yo te quiero infinito
yo te acuerda oh mi corazón
Spanish bombs, yo te quiero infinito
yo te acuerda oh mi corazón

Spanish songs in Andalucia, Mandolina, oh mi corazón
Spanish songs in Granada, oh mi corazón.
'Spanish Bombs' – Written by Joe Strummer, Mick Jones, Paul Gustave
Simonon and Topper Headon.

After Strummer and his fellow bandmember Paul Simonon sacked guitarist, singer and songwriter Mick Jones in 1983, The Clash began to fall apart, and Strummer sought refuge in Granada.

Strummer was in Spain when critics panned 'This is England', the single from the band's final album, *Cut the Crap*. Talking after the event, he stated that on hearing the reviews: 'I just went, "Well fuck this," and fucked off to the mountains of Spain to sit sobbing under a palm tree.' If you ask me, it's a great song

Strummer's premature death in 2002, along with a reappraisal of his cultural significance, led to a Facebook campaign to persuade the city authorities of Granada to name a city square after him.

In May 2013, Placeta Joe Strummer was inaugurated in the Realejo quarter by his widow and several hundred fans. The small square is adorned with a mural of Strummer, by street artist El Niño de las Pinturas.

Not for the first time, or the last, I told the boys about my meetings with Joe Strummer. We paid our respects. We sang some songs.

Joe Strummer, The Clash, a soundtrack to the past.

A LIFE OF SURPRISES
Granada, Chite and Malaga

That Was Then

We walked, or more accurately stumbled, back towards Plaza Santa Ana. I crossed a road without looking. Brakes screeched. A taxi stopped just in time. I thought that I'd be the subject of justified vilification, but the taxi driver just smiled and offered us a lift. Speaking in Spanish, he explained that he had a young family, but he had little money. Business was bad. He'd been driving around for ages, with an empty cab. He'd been praying for the chance to earn a fare. Suddenly we appeared in the middle of the street, as if from nowhere, as if by magic, as if by divine intervention. He said a 'Hail Mary', before crossing himself and kissing a crucifix which swung loosely from the rear-view mirror of his car.

I didn't think that I'd ever been the answer to anyone's prayers before. I checked with Ariana, just to make sure. She confirmed that I probably hadn't. It was a sobering thought. I probably never would be again.

The taxi driver continued to smile broadly. He couldn't have been more cheerful. He was almost ecstatic. His faith had been confirmed.

La Movida may have begun, but traditional values and religion still had a firm grip on Spain. For the most part, the country was a God-fearing nation. Perhaps this may explain the superstitious nature of the Spanish people.

Superstition was a word originally used to mean the opposite of religion, the decorous and pious worship of the gods. The Roman scholar Varro distinguished between the superstitious man, who feared the gods as his enemies, and the religious man, who was devoted to them as his parents. But, whilst the Roman Catholic Church may preach against what it defines as superstition – false beliefs and charms – faith itself can also be seen as a form of superstition – it's just a matter of perspective. One man's religion is another man's superstition. When you believe in things you don't understand, you may feel blessed, but you may also suffer.

Tonight, I'd been the answer to somebody's prayers, but on other occasions in Spain, I'd acted as a harbinger of bad luck.

Silent screams greeted my greetings of salutation performed with a glass of water. The Spanish believe that making a toast is like offering a gift up to God. Obviously, God would be very disappointed with a simple glass of water and therefore would shower down bad luck on anyone who offered such a disappointing beverage. Some people believe that such a mistake can lead to seven years of bad sex – an issue upon which you'll hear no comment from me. Another faux pas, which caused raised eyebrows, was when I joined in a toast but stared at my glass. If you don't look people in the eye while toasting, you are once again bringing bad luck to all and sundry. Spilling wine (or salt for that matter) is another no-no. I've seen people anointing themselves with their remaining unspilled wine and crossing themselves furiously.

Forget Friday the 13th, in Spain the unluckiest day is Tuesday the 13th. Toast someone with water, whilst not looking them in the eye and knocking over some wine on a Tuesday, which happens to be the 13th day of the month, and you might as well leave the country while the going's still good.

Another no-no: don't ever buy anyone yellow clothes as a gift, as you'll be given the evil eye; superstition dictates that you shouldn't give anyone yellow clothing, as this is very definitely bad luck. This supposedly comes from the idea that the colour represents sulphur and the Devil.

Also, don't buy family or friends something that cuts as a gift, such as knives or scissors; tradition says that this means that the relationship will be broken.

Speaking of friends, when I was initially contemplating busking, a Spanish friend suddenly said '*mucha mierda*' or 'much shit'. I thought that he'd heard me play, but apparently the phrase is akin to saying, 'break a leg' – he was wishing me good luck.

Sitting in the back of the taxi, I had a chance to reflect upon my good luck – I hadn't been run over for one thing. Here I was, I thought. Enjoying a hedonistic, pleasure seeking lifestyle, which I knew wouldn't last forever (the days were slipping away) but which I was determined to enjoy. I'd come to Spain, searching for a life-changing experience, but I'd come to realise that life didn't need to change in any great or significant way, although perhaps my attitude to life did. I'd fallen for Spain, more than I could possibly have imagined, but if my life had changed in any real way at all, it was in the realisation that life is about living, giving and sharing multiple experiences – it's not about that one moment, that one thing, that quest for the out of reach, the intangible, the unobtainable. There's no point seeking a life-changing experience, there's just a life that changes. Whatever life throws at you, you've got to make the most of it.

As I got out of the cab, I realised that a lot of the 'stuff' that I think about is rubbish. But, with a profound sense of relief, and an appreciation of my good fortune, I went to bed and slept soundly.

Tomorrow would be another day.

THIS IS NOW

The roads around Granada may have improved considerably, but the local buses are still fairly slow. I came to this conclusion whilst waiting at yet another bus stop on our tour of just about every bus stop in every village between Granada and Chite. At this particular bus stop, the driver disembarked, but not before locking the door of the bus. He disappeared for what seemed like ages. A lunch stop, a smoking stop, a shagging stop? Who really knew what he was up to?

To cut a long journey short, we arrived back in Chite far later than expected. It was our last night in the small town so we were determined to make the most of it. We cleaned ourselves up, changed and then dropped down to see Stuart and Olwyn. They informed us that tonight, Chite would be hosting a small summer fiesta – things were looking up. Stuart then told us that they were heading out to meet some friends at the agricultural bar, which we were reliably informed was open – did we want to join them? Not being ones to turn down a drink or good company, we tagged along.

We strolled towards Chite's main square, chatting all the way. As we approached the bar, a man and two women turned to face us. They were standing beside a few rickety chairs and tables which had been set up outside the bar. I had the distinct impression that I knew at least one of Stuart and Olwyn's friends – I'd seen that face somewhere before. 'Peter, Elaine, Cecily, meet Andy and Tania, and Will and Tom.' Peter was none other than Peter Capaldi, aka Doctor Who and Malcolm Tucker. He was staying in Chite with his wife, TV producer Elaine Collins, and their daughter Cecily. Although only irregular visitors to the area, they'd built up a friendship with Stuart, who'd previously collected them from the airport.

The Capaldis are a charming family. They were both interesting and interested. Tom couldn't quite believe that Doctor Who was asking him about his ambition to become a doctor. However, *Doctor Who*, the programme, was the proverbial white elephant in the room. Reluctant to talk about showbusiness, TV and film, we avoided the obvious conversations. Avoided, that is, until Tom mentioned *Skins* and I felt comfortable enough to bring up Malcolm Tucker and *The Thick of It*.

Who would have thought it? Showbusiness in Chite. But things were about to get even stranger and more unbelievable. Another couple arrived at the bar and joined our table. Peter and one of the new arrivals became engaged in a conversation about music – likes and dislikes, etc. The talk turned to '80s music, familiar ground for me – home territory, if you like. I joined in the conversation, quietly declaring my love of indie music, The Smiths and Postcard Records. Elaine leant across and whispered, 'You know who that is, don't you?' 'No,' I replied. 'It's Dr Robert from the Blow Monkeys.' I was shocked, excited and surprised. I was a fan back in the day. That probably explains why I involuntarily jumped, spilt my wine and shouted 'Forget Doctor Who, I've met Dr Robert.' I guess that it didn't have to be that way, but the elephant in the room was unveiled. The elephant in the room was well and truly up for discussion. The night of the two doctors had commenced.

We chatted, long into the night. We talked about film, acting, producing, teaching, politics, family, music, The Smiths, *Top of the Pops*, guitars and Spain;

the fiesta provided a backdrop to conversation. It's nights like these, when everything unfolds in an unplanned and surprisingly pleasant way, that create the very best times and the very best memories. If we had been staying in Chite for a few more days, we would have been able to attend a party at which the two doctors 'jammed'. Sweet music indeed. Life has a habit of springing up interesting surprises. Life can be both ordinary and extraordinary – if you celebrate both, then you can't go too far wrong.

We said our goodbyes and walked home at about 2:00 a.m. The night and day had been long – almost as long as the spirit measures which ensured a sound night's sleep. Our celebrity evening had become a celebration of our holiday. It was going to be hard to get up in the morning – I wasn't even sure that I wanted to leave. Time would tell.

With little choice in the morning but to move on, we started driving towards Malaga. However, a certain amount of late-night alcohol-induced tiredness initiated a decision to stop off at what turned out to be a very lovely little beach. Located just to the east of Almunecar, Playa de Cabria is approached via a bumpy and potholed dirt track. The approach could have been better, but the unspoilt black sand and shingle beaches were a delight. Two beaches, both with gently shelving profiles, led down to a warm sea. The beaches were connected by a short causeway. Our decision to stop was fairly spur-of-the-moment, but it delivered more than a moment's worth of promise. We stayed for longer than anticipated. We even found time to hire a kayak. We provided most our own entertainment, but the beach also provided some of its own. As we lounged, a slightly shifty-looking man was arrested by two none-too-gentle policemen, right in front of us. He resisted arrest, but resistance was futile. Shortly afterwards, a woman in a beautiful and elegant wedding dress suddenly appeared on the beach – she dived into the sea, fully clothed – a matrimonial ritual, a celebration or a matrimonial failure? It was impossible to know or understand. It all happens in Spain. We put everything down to experience, stored up the experiences and moved on.

That Was Then

Tomorrow was another day, but the days were running out. When I'd arrived in Spain, the days and weeks appeared to be endless, and for a while at least time lost its meaning, as one day joyfully drifted into another. Then I reached that stage where the number of days past was equal to the number of days left before a return to the UK beckoned. From that point onwards, time speeded up exponentially.

Life continued to be lived in a similar way, but perhaps at greater speed and perhaps ever more frantically. We enjoyed, we indulged and we took advantage of all that Granada had to offer. Clubs, restaurants, cinemas, shows, cafes and bars – always bars. I felt like I was becoming more Spanish, more cosmopolitan – I ate late, I enjoyed good food, I knew how to enjoy myself and I lived in the shadows. I felt European, but my language skills were limited – Ariana naturally took the lead in conversations, but when it came to ordering drinks I was practically bilingual.

Time may have been running out, but I'd had a fantastic time and I was determined to make the most of what little time still remained. I spent my last few days in Granada, revisiting favourite haunts. The nightclub in a cave house, the Alhambra, a forgotten but fantastic bar that caused queues to form just because it uniquely sold toasted sandwiches made in a 'Breville' toaster, the Plaza Nueva, the Plaza Santa Ana, the Albaicin, the Mirador San Nicolas, and a quite delightful cafe which sold the very best chocolate and churros I'd ever tasted. There was much that I would miss, but I'd made friends, I'd had adventures, I'd busked, I'd read Hemingway, I'd met Joe Strummer, I'd fallen in love with life and I now more clearly than ever understood just how much more the world has to offer than the limitations imposed by introspective patriotism, borders and a fear of the outside. Travel not only broadens the mind, but it widens our horizons and raises our spirits – travel broadens our outlook on life.

THIS IS NOW

I didn't really know what to expect from Malaga. I'd only stayed there once before, and while one night spent in a dodgy hotel and a brothel in 1984 might not be representative of Malaga today, I had limited expectations.

We arrived straight from the beach. We'd booked a room at the Novotel Suites. We were dishevelled and slightly sandy, but we weren't turned away. The hotel was modern and modular, almost 'space age' in design. The rooms were impressive – large, bright and very contemporary. They cleverly utilised space: everything was hidden away, but easy to find – a microwave oven, a sink, a fridge, many wardrobes and a TV with a free selection of recent movies. There were plenty of shelves, extra hanging spaces and a hidden space for suitcases. The living room area included a coffee table which rose up to become a dining table or desk at the press of a button. The bathroom was small, but included a bath and a separate shower. Power points were everywhere, as were electrical switches. From the bed, you could control all the lighting and various other gadgets in the room. However, what was perhaps most impressive of all (considering my last stay in Malaga) was the fact that our room included several floor to ceiling windows – it was nice to finally have a room with a view.

The view was quite impressive. It included the sea and the city centre, which was only about ten minutes away. Tania and I were inspired, the boys less so. It took a while to persuade them to accompany us and to leave the TV and all the gadgets alone, but eventually we set out to explore Malaga.

There's actually much more to Malaga than one might at first expect. The birthplace of Picasso, it is the sixth largest city in Spain, and it has one of the longest histories of any city in Spain. Malaga was founded by the Phoenicians as Malaka, in 770 BC. The name probably derives from the Phoenician word for 'salt' – fish was salted close by. From the 6th century BC, the city found itself dominated by Carthage. Then, from 218 BC, it was ruled by the Roman Republic and later the Roman Empire as Malaca. After the fall of the Roman Empire and the end of Visigothic rule, it came under Islamic rule for 800 years, until the Crown of Castile gained control during the Reconquista. The fall of Malaga in 1487, to Christian forces, made the fall of Granada an inevitable reality. The Muslim inhabitants of Malaga had successfully resisted assaults and artillery bombardments until hunger finally forced them to surrender; virtually the entire population was sold into slavery or given as 'gifts' to other Christian rulers.

Violence was to erupt again during the Spanish Civil War. During the initial stages of the conflict, the Spanish Republic retained control of Malaga – its harbour was a base for the Spanish Republican Navy. As previously mentioned, Malaga suffered heavy bombardment and shelling by Francoist forces because of its importance to the Republican cause, before finally being subjugated and forced to bear witness to a terrible massacre perpetrated by the Nationalists.

We headed towards the heart of the city. It was a real revelation. Grand modern buildings, linked by canvas awnings, concealed a historic core. The city was a delight – styled and stylised, it was a lovely place to be. Shops, museums, the cathedral, churches, parks, monuments, a Roman theatre and Moorish fortresses, all neatly packed into to a relatively small area. Malaga is an interesting mixture of ancient and modern, the architecture contrasts, but at the same time it compliments in a quite magnificent way.

We headed towards Malaga's most important landmark, the Alcazaba. It's one of two Moorish fortresses found in the city, the other being the Gibralfaro. The fortress's entrance is close to the Plaza de Aduana and the Roman theatre; it forms part of the city walls. We passed through the Puerta de la Bóveda (Gate of the Vault), a typical Moorish defensive doorway designed to delay any attack or any attackers. Entering through an arch, approaching enemy forces would have come face to face with a solid and sheer wall – corralled and confused they would have been exposed and vulnerable to counterattack by boiling water or possibly boiling oil.

As we moved higher we passed through the Puerta de la Columnas (Gate of the Columns), which was built using Roman marble columns to hold up Moorish horseshoe arches. From here we entered the lower levels of the Alcazaba, via another defensive doorway situated beneath the Torre del Cristo (Christ's Tower). This was where the first Mass was celebrated following the victory over the town by the Catholic monarchs.

We could sense the history of place – the bricks, blocks and mortar of the Alcazaba have many stories to tell. We followed the contours of the hill, stopping to explore some of the building's outer defensive walls and resting for a while in some quite charming gardens. Then, following a cobbled path, we entered the higher levels of the fortress and the Nazari Palace. We explored courtyards and gardens, marvelling at the many glorious arches and wonderful fountains. The views from the battlements were impressive and expansive – all the way up to the Gibralfaro, and down to the city centre, the bullring, the harbour and the sea.

The Gibralfaro is situated above the Alcazaba, but it's connected to it by a fortified double walled walkway. It was here in the Gibralfaro, after a three-month siege by the forces of Ferdinand and Isabella, that the Muslim defenders were finally forced to surrender. The fall of Malaga removed any possibility of reinforcements arriving from North Africa – Muslim Granada was now isolated and alone – its days as a Muslim stronghold were numbered – the Reconquista was almost complete.

Our first exploration of the city was almost complete, but we decided to make a little detour – we decided to walk back to our hotel by way of the harbour. As we headed down in the general direction of the sea, we encountered the elegant, palm-shaded Paseo del Parque. This area, which runs parallel to the seafront, is not only a charming walkway, but it's also a quite remarkable botanical garden. Hundreds of exotic plants and flowers delight the eye, while your ears and eyes are drawn to the screech of the parakeets which nest at the very top of the tall palms. We marvelled at all the wonderful sights, sounds, scents and colours, before crossing over to the seafront itself.

Until fairly recently, Malaga's port was off-limits to members of the public. But it's been recently regenerated and redesigned, and the developments have been spectacularly successful.

With sparkling sea, luxury yachts and huge cruise ships on one side, and designer shops, themed bars, restaurants and the 'Pompidou Centre' on the other side, we contentedly strolled along the wide and elegantly redesigned waterfront walkway – we may have stopped for a mojito or two, but we generally kept moving. We were surprised and impressed by the mix of graceful architecture and genuinely spectacular views – we obviously weren't the only ones. The area is a popular spot. People of all ages paraded up and down and then back again – families, couples, the young, the very young, the old, the romantic, the pragmatic, locals, tourists, the lost, the lonely and the occasional jogger.

We strolled without intent or intended direction, but we found ourselves heading towards a lighthouse and the Playa de la Malagueta. We emerged onto a wide, gently sloping, sand and shingle beach. It looked like nature at its best, but the beach is man-made. One side of the beach is protected by a series of huge boulders or 'rock armour' – the hard engineering protects not only the coast, but also a colony of cats. The crevices and cracks are home to many of Malaga's strays.

The beach began to empty as a gentle breeze announced the forthcoming end of the day. We gazed out to sea and into the land. Darkness intensified. The sun began to set. Boats became silhouettes, as the harbour lights and streets lights shimmered. The lure and the lull of the sea was intense. We spoke in hushed whispers. I love the beach at this time of day, as the crowds invariably depart and peace and quiet reign supreme. We reflected on our holiday and upon our good fortune. We rejoiced and embraced amidst an atmosphere of relaxed reflection. Everything was perfect – everything was calm – as calm as the waves that gently lapped at our feet.

It was time to head for home.

That Was Then

Engines revved as middle-aged women cried, some wailed. Hollow-faced shaven-headed young men either looked for comfort or looked to the floor. There were emotional embraces, heartfelt conversations and long, distant silences. Extreme sadness, grief, future loss and separation were prevailing sentiments, but they were dealt with in different ways.

I thought I was sad to be leaving Granada, but my sadness couldn't compete or compare. It was as nothing compared to the anguish of this group of Spanish mothers who were about to lose their sons to the military.

We were in a coach station, but I'd never seen such raw emotion and deep-felt sorrow. For most of the women, tears were not enough. For most of the raw recruits, their fears were more than enough. Conscription was alive and kicking and had been a military tradition in Spain, since 1770.

Thankful that I was heading back to the UK rather than joining the army, I reappraised my situation. I was sad to be leaving Granada, but I'd had an amazing time – I had my memories and I'd be back.

I grabbed my bag, said a quick prayer (I hadn't forgotten the mountain roads) and found a seat on the Malaga-bound coach.

As we pulled out of the coach station, I took one long last look at the city.

Who was I kidding? I could hear the Moor's sigh.

THIS IS NOW

Social media often gets a bad press; this could be due to the fact that social media often makes the traditional role of the press an irrelevance. Where Twitter and Facebook lead, the press often follows. To my mind, the expansion of social media is a largely positive phenomenon. More often than not breaking news is now in the hands of the people: surely this is a step in the right direction. However, with great power, comes great responsibility. Today, media companies line up to secure stories from their new and largely untapped horde of free, freelance journalists. News is instant, communication is global, and stories that have relevance to the masses are able to be accessed by the masses before they are given priority by the press.

At an individual level, social media bestows on us the ability to stay in touch with friends (both old and new) from all over the world. Twitter, Facebook, Instagram – where else can you meet so easily with likeminded (and not so likeminded) individuals and groups? Sharing experiences, thoughts and ideas? How else can you so easily stay in touch with distant friends?

In distant times, days often began with a frantic search for a cigarette. Today, we are much more likely to wake up and reach for our iPhones or our Androids – social media is as addictive, if not more addictive than nicotine.

I woke. I yawned. I Facebooked.

I admired an old school friend's artistic prowess, I grew angry about some right-wing revisionism – 'No, Thatcher wasn't a visionary' – I smiled as some cats did some mildly amusing things, I completed a quiz, which informed me that I should get out more often, and I noticed that a friend from university, who I hadn't seen for over ten years, was staying just down the road.

A couple of messages later and I'd arranged to meet John Gregory in Malaga.

On holiday with his son and two daughters, John was and is a great friend. He'd do anything for anyone and when you're around him, things have a habit of happening – he creates opportunities and openings. In days gone by we'd shared drinks, late nights and a competitive interest in backgammon – I'd 'smuggled' John into France, together we'd run a nightclub, and it was through John that I met Joe Strummer for a second time.

In May 1985, the original Clash line-up was no more. 'Clash 2', minus Mick Jones and Topper Headon, decided to get back to basics. They were fed up with venues charging overinflated prices for their gigs. Inspired by an idea from their manager, Joe Strummer and the rest of the band embarked on a busking tour of Britain. Taking their acoustic guitars with them, but leaving their wallets and anything else of value behind, they hitched, busked and blagged their way around several northern towns and cities.

I dropped around to see John, one lazy afternoon when we were both living in Leeds. We chatted briefly, before I asked if I could use his loo. 'Sorry mate,' he replied. 'Joe Strummer's in the toilet.'

Strange but true.

John met the band while they were busking in Leeds city centre. When he found out that they didn't have anywhere to stay, he naturally invited them to stay at his.

That evening, as I watched The Clash busk outside the University Union building, I found it hard to believe that I'd met Joe Strummer for a second time. It was only a year since our last encounter. He claimed to remember, but I wasn't entirely sure.

What I was sure about, however, was the fact that I was looking forward to meeting up with John. But before our much-anticipated reunion, there were a couple of places that we wanted to see and a couple of things that we wanted to do.

Our first destination was Malaga Cathedral. Originally built in 1528, the cathedral has never officially been completed – it lacks a tower on the west front. While original plans allowed for two towers to be built, a radical bishop donated the available funds to the American cause during the American War of Independence. Consequently, the cathedral is often affectionately referred to as La Manquita, or 'the one-armed woman'. We ventured inside. We were impressed by the sheer scale of the building and the soaring vertical columns.

Our next stop was the Picasso Museum. Located just around the corner from the cathedral, the museum is housed in an impressive 16th-century palace. The museum itself houses an impressive collection of some of Picasso's lesser-known works, both early and modern. It was also home to a temporary exhibition of some of Jackson Pollock's work – if I'm honest, I was more interested in the black and white photos which inspired his work, rather than the work itself.

From the museum we moved onto and into Casa Lola – a quite delightful little bar, selling great wine and delicious food. Loud, noisy, busy and frantic – it was our kind of place. We enjoyed lovely tapas and *pinxtos* – the *pil pil* prawns, Iberian *hamburguesas*, *flamenquins* and croquettes were particularly good.

Full of food and full of culture, we headed off to meet John in the Paseo del Parque. One of the real signs of friendship is that time spent apart loses any real relevance. It may have been over ten years since we'd last met, but in under ten minutes we were as thick as thieves. We spent the rest of the day with John and his delightful children – Olivia, Sophie and Thomas. We headed to the port and back to the beach – we talked, we laughed, we reminisced and we drank 'buckets' of beer.

We couldn't have had a better last night in Spain.

FINAL THOUGHTS

That Was Then

'It is a truth universally acknowledged, that a young man in possession of time, must inevitably waste it.'

We arrived at the airport with plenty of time to spare – thankfully, the coach hadn't broken down en route or plunged over a precipice. With so much time to spare we pulled up some chairs and settled down for a drink. We ruminated and we reminisced. We talked about Spain, and we talked about home. We pondered our past our present and our future.

I may not have found that life-changing experience, but I felt like I'd successfully immersed myself in the Spain of Hemingway, Laurie Lee and Orwell. I also felt like I'd walked in the shadow of Lorca, Durruti and La Pasionaria. I was intoxicated by and with Spain, but I didn't want to get too intoxicated before the flight home.

One drink became two – time lost its relevance. Two drinks became three – I lost my relevance.

Perhaps it was time to check in?

I sauntered up to the desk and handed over my ticket. The lady at the check-in desk looked concerned – she glanced at a clock on the wall and then handed back my ticket with a worried frown.

'Señor – usted se ha equivocado de aeropuerto.'

Well, as it turned out, I wasn't exactly in the wrong airport, but I was in the wrong terminal, and the right one was a in a completely different building. My ticket said London, but I'd failed to notice that my return flight flew via Madrid – I was in the international departures lounge waiting for a domestic flight.

Panic ensued. A taxi was called. A rush and a push and I was on my way.

There wasn't time for goodbyes.

THIS IS NOW

Another rude awakening, another alarm call.

It's never a good thing to be shocked into consciousness, but we were up and out of the hotel pretty quickly – unfortunately, the journey to the airport

didn't go quite so quickly. Slowed, confused, hindered and irritated by a faulty satnav system and Malaga's one-way system, it seemed to take an age until we finally reached the airport. At this point we thought our troubles were over, but although we'd found the airport we couldn't find the drop-off point for the car. We ended up circling the airport in 'never' decreasing circles – to an observer it must have looked like we were being held in a holding pattern.

Thankfully, we spotted a half-hidden sign on a half-hidden side road – things couldn't have been made much more difficult if they'd tried – perhaps they had? Unfortunately, our relief was short-lived. The sign accurately directed us to the wrong parking bay. Down but not out, we swallowed our pride and asked for directions. Heeding proffered advice, we drove the wrong way around a large underground car park, narrowly avoiding several oncoming vehicles, until we finally found an 'Auto Navarro' sign.

Fear of flying has got nothing on my new-found fear of parking. Nerves were frayed.

We took a few moments to compose ourselves before unloading and then handing over the hire car. Grabbing our cases, we headed swiftly towards the international departures terminal – I double-checked our tickets. Once inside we joined a long queue which snaked towards the check-in desk – I checked our tickets again.

As the queue inched forward, I heard a distinctive voice rise above the general murmur of the crowd. 'I can't find anybody here who speaks English. Bloody awful this place.' The owner of the voice was an elderly grey-haired gentleman. Dapperly dressed, he pontificated about life, the universe and Spain. Looking like an ageing Lothario, he reclined on his luggage trolley and moaned to anyone who cared to listen.

I didn't care to listen, but I didn't have a choice. The Lothario wandered up and started chatting. We didn't have a conversation as such, but he moaned in my general direction. I discovered that the Lothario had been living in Spain for two months, whilst looking for somewhere to live, but his xenophobic outpourings argued against residence – he'd also been looking in Gibraltar, but claimed that it was full of Spaniards. 'No English,' he insisted, 'I didn't even see a bloody monkey. Got bitten by every insect in the world.' His views on Spain, the Spanish and Europeans were the antithesis of mine.

I stopped myself from saying something that I knew I might regret – perhaps I shouldn't have done. I think the ageing Lothario realised that I didn't really want to listen and I think he recognised my growing antipathy. Still moaning, he wandered off in search of another victim. I saw him heading towards the boarding gate, where he appeared to be trying to chat up a young woman – perhaps he'd bought some Viagra at duty free.

Spain's loss, England's gain? I didn't think so.

The queue edged forward. We reached the check in desk and handed over our tickets – they weren't returned. We picked up our boarding cards and headed towards passport control. Our holiday was almost over.

I reflected on our trip – I'd wanted a holiday, not a life-changing experience, but in many ways this holiday was more life-changing than my trip in 1984.

Whilst we'd been staying in Chite, we'd looked at a house in Niguelas, and we'd made an offer. Whilst driving to the airport, we'd been informed that our offer had been accepted.

I looked around. I wanted to live here. Well, not in the airport (I'd never be able to park), but definitely in Spain.

A life that changes. We were departing, we were leaving, but it many ways it felt like a new beginning.

Perhaps our dream would become a reality.